Praise for Author J.

Empowered to move forward...

Jacqui is such a powerful presence, who challenges your thinking, while at the same time putting you at ease with her kindness and genuineness. I was able to identify and destroy some shockingly cruel core beliefs about myself that were lurking under the surface undetected. I really appreciated the silent pauses she uses to allow me to have breakthroughs. Through the sessions with her I gained clarity and felt empowered to move forward in my career and personal life. I would love to be coached by Jacqui in the future if I feel stuck again.

-   **Caroline Delaney**

Asking the right questions...

Jacqui is a fabulous coach. She has really helped me to find my own answers, by asking the right questions! She is very encouraging and engaging. She believed in me that I could take the right steps in my professional career. I found Jacqui very easy to work with and I would highly recommend her.

-   **S.**

1

Clarity...

Thank you very much Jacqui for your amazing coaching. Your guidance gave me great clarity on which direction to go in the future for work and career.

- **Marie Fleming**

Mindset changes can make a big difference...

A recent session with Jacqui helped me to achieve clarity around my goals. Jacqui's warm, friendly and professional approach made me feel at ease and she gave me lots of useful tips to take away after the session. I would recommend Jacqui as a life coach.

After we spoke I've never felt lighter!! It's been amazing not to have that feeling anymore. I didn't realise how much it consumed me and my daily thoughts.

I'd never been to life coaching before so wasn't sure what to expect but soon realised that mindset changes can make big differences very quickly!

It's clear that Jacqui loves her job and genuinely cares about her client's wellbeing, recommended to anyone looking to improve and better their lives in just a few small steps.

- **H. K.**

Seek the answers...

I had a number sessions with Jacqui as I was going through what I would call a very confusing time in my life. I was feeling very confused and completely lost my focus on who I was and where I was going. I never thought for one minute that when I sent that initial appointment request that after just two sessions I would feel so empowered and like a huge weight would be lifted.

To be honest I was shocked at how one question Jacqui asked me during one of my sessions and the answer I gave had such a positive impact on me and how at that very moment I could almost hear the penny drop in my head.... It all became clear. At times the silence was awkward but that is part of the process as I did more of the talking and realised I actually had all the answers myself. Jacqui was there to encourage and guide me to seek the answers for myself as she knew I had them...as everyone sometimes just needs a nudge to dig deep and find them.

I also learned another very important life lesson seeking help from a professional when life gets tough is not weak in fact it's one of the strongest things you can do.

Wishing you every success xx

- **Louise O'Hanlon**

INSPIRE, HEAL, EMPOWER

About the Book

This is my story, in 1984 at the age of 15 years old, I was admitted for an eye operation into a busy hospital. Whilst in hospital I was made undergo, without my consent, what I would for many years call an inappropriate medical examination. It has taken some 37 years for me to break the silence that surrounds that day and give what happened to me its correct title and name - sexual assault.

I also share some of my personal writings, poems and the tools that I use and which are intended to INSPIRE, HEAL & EMPOWER others.

My wish is to give you an insight into my personal journey and how I've dealt with and overcome the impact and effects of the sexual assault that was done to me on that day. I encourage you, regardless of your age, to listen to that part of yourself that instinctively knows what is right and what is best for you, I call it 'Your Absolute Knowing' - that part of us that so many have not been taught or encouraged to listen to.

With my life experiences and my coaching skills I have been able to finally look at, deal with and work through the mental and emotional challenges that trauma caused. And to let it go back to who it truly belongs to, the person who chose to sexually assault a 15 year old girl.

In sharing my story, breaking the silence and talking about an often unspoken topic I am now shining a light on a dark moment with others. In shining this light on my own dark places the deep shame that I took on that day and carried for years has now disappeared - gone away, packed its bags and left!

My wish is the same for you if you are effected by any of the subject matter within this book.

Jacqui Taaffe

www.JacquiTaaffe.com

About the Author

'I realise in writing this book that the time is right NOW and how inspiring, healing and empowering it has been to go through this process - to write, journal, create images and write poems with the intention of sharing my story with you, the reader.

I can't stress enough the benefit of the writing and reflection process and how it has helped me to NOW share my story, to break the silence, to free myself from shame and to stand into my power.

The time is NOW.'

Jacqui Taaffe is an Executive life coach, mentor, facilitator and speaker, with over 25 years managerial experience in the development and progression of people, Jacqui specialises in working alongside people to develop their mindset and better mental health habits to improve their lives.

Passionate about creating awareness with people by enabling them to look at the thoughts, stories and beliefs that they tell themselves because these create their reality, Jacqui knows from experience that when you become an authority on yourself; on your thoughts, beliefs and behaviours you are then able to step into your power - that is self-empowerment.

At her therapy clinic Jacqui provides 1:1 consultations and coach's people to change their mindset and create change in their life. Jacqui continues to expand her services including Hypnotherapy and Mind Coaching.

Jacqui is also a bereavement counsellor volunteer with a wonderful local bereavement counselling service since 2018 and she finds it personally hugely rewarding.

JacquiTaaffe.com

Facebook.com/JTCoaching007/

Twitter.com/taaffe_jacqui

LinkedIn: Jacqui Taaffe

Instagram.com/jt_coaching_jacqui_taaffe_/

INSPIRE, HEAL, EMPOWER

A TRUE STORY OF FINDING YOUR VOICE

BREAKING THE SILENCE &

TRUSTING ONE'S KNOWING

BY JACQUI TAAFFE

Jacqui Taaffe Publishing

This book is dedicated to Pat and Kara

For Pat

<u>The Rock</u>

He is the rock

I have been allowed to stand upon,

He is the unmoving foundation which

Allows me to be myself.

He is silent, supportive,

A constant presence I know

I can rest my head and lean upon

He is steadfast, he holds

Our worries, he silently

Keeps them to himself.

He is incredible and he doesn't see it

He is gentle and most incredible of all is

His humbleness because he

Seeks no credit, no recognition

He just provides a safe space which

He constantly gives.

Who is he?

Who is the Rock you might ask?

That Rock is my husband Pat, and this poem

I dedicate to him.

- Jacqui Taaffe, July 2020

For Kara

Thank you for the wonderful eye illustration and for your encouragements.

As I finished writing this book, as any author will understand, I had to prepare myself to share it publicly. This is at times a difficult, exciting and disconcerting experience.

Kara turned to me one day and gave me the insight and wisdom that I needed to hear in that moment and reminded me of my reason for writing this book as she said to me; 'Mum you mightn't like what I am going to say. You know people are going to judge you but what's more important is to share your story to help others.'

For Jacqui

I first heard Jacqui touch on the subject of this book, what she called back then – 'an event that happened to her,' when she gave a presentation on herself and her life on The Outstanding Network at the start of May 2020.

I did not know it then but Jacqui had already identified me as the person who would help her to write this book. It has been a privilege to share this journey with Jacqui and to help her tell her story and share it in this way.

Over some 8 months I have watched Jacqui become increasingly comfortable with sharing her story and talk about what happened to her. In particular observing how, as she lost her discomfort and became more able to name what had happened to her and talk about it, how others around her were able to listen and hear her story without pity or discomfort.

Because of her strength and acceptance and through the process of writing this book I have witnessed Jacqui grow in her ability to openly talk about her own experiences and how she has truly overcome them. Jacqui is also open about the fact that she still regularly uses the tools and exercises within this book. In her acceptance and openness Jacqui inspires feelings of connection and trust in those around her.

It has been a time of great joy to work with Jacqui to write this book and share it with you.

Heather Shields

Heather Shields Publishing

Editor, January 2021

Contents

Chapter One Looking and Seeing......................23

Chapter Two This is only part of my story........33

Chapter Three Absolute Deep Knowing............51

Chapter Four Shame.......................................59

Chapter Five I Eye..79

Chapter Six Justice and Judgement 89

Chapter Seven It's not my story to keep.........103

Chapter Eight Cleaning Up 111

Chapter Nine My Right to Choose 119

Chapter 10 The Power of Enough 133

Chapter 11 Rising Choices 143

Chapter 12 Enough is Enough 153

Postscript...165

INSPIRE, HEAL, EMPOWER TOOLKIT 173

Chapter One

Looking and Seeing

The man appeared at the door of my hospital room, I was 15 years old and alone and in hospital for an eye operation. Standing in his white coat this man, who I believed was a doctor, told me he was there to examine me. 'Ok I said,' sitting up in my hospital gown.

The man walked over to the bed and after pulling the curtains around me, told me that he needed to perform an internal examination. I felt stunned and a cold numbness ran through my body. I knew instinctively this didn't feel right, it felt really, really wrong and I immediately challenged him. A shy, naïve 15 year-old girl but my gut told me this is wrong. I asked; 'What's that got to do with my eye?'

Staring me down he said with cold authority, 'It needs to be done.'

He told me to lie back on the bed for the examination. I felt completely sick, stunned and a suffocating pressure on my chest. I remember feeling closed in by him and the hospital curtains that should have protected me were instead used to hide a sexual assault by him that I would carry silently for the next 26 years before I started to resolve them and it has taken me a further 11 years to unfold, heal and become empowered from the events of that day. In this book I will share with you my story of what happened that day and its immediate and subsequent impact on me. I will also share how I finally came to speak about this event (sexual assault) and start to look directly at that day.

More importantly I want to share with you the lessons that I have learned and the tools that I have found and used to change my story for me. I have become inspired, healed and empowered and I wish the same for anyone else who this resonates with, in whatever way.

Now, almost 37 years later I still use the tools that I have learned over the past decade and I see the huge shifts and progress that I have been able to make with this knowledge and information.

As a consequence of the sexual assault I felt shame and carried it silently for many years. In recent years I have been able to hand that shame back to the man who did this to me. I may never know who he was, I do not need to know that and I certainly don't want to know why he did it as it is clear that was his intention - I could have been anyone that day, it just happened to be me in that hospital bed. In 2014, I made a statement to the Gardaí and made a full disclosure of the events of that day, a Garda came to my home and we sat at my kitchen table. Many months later the same Garda rang me to let me know that they had carried out a formal investigation in the hospital but due to lack of documentation and evidence the Office of the Director of Public Prosecutions, DPP, could not proceed with the investigation. On reflection, I had to let go of any belief that he might be found, I believed that to focus there would be a complete waste of my headspace, time and energy. It is enough for me that I can now hand the shame and everything else back to him and no longer carry the painful legacy of that day. I have empowered myself by letting go of the Swamp-like figure that appeared at the side of my hospital bed because searching for him would only be giving my power away.

In looking at the sexual assault and both his and my behaviour in those few minutes I have learned so much about how one copes with trauma and power dynamics. Through my own journey of personal development and by using coaching tools I have inspired, healed and empowered myself to stand up as a beacon of light. I have reconsidered labels of victims and survivors and believe we must first make the choice whether we want to be labelled or not. If so, what label would you choose? I wanted a label that empowered me and I chose beacon of light because I have found that when I shine a light on silence and difficult conversations I am empowered. When I found an organisation that was working with people who had suffered sexual abuse or inappropriate sexual behaviour whilst a patient in a hospital I began to understand that I wasn't alone and my feelings of emptiness were only a symptom of something I had been through.

Looking at where I am now and my journey to get here I want to be a beacon of light for others and through my personal reflections in this book share all that I have come to understand and learn with someone else.

'We must feel content
in giving consent.'

It has also raised for me the issue of Consent and the importance of seeking and giving consent. We must feel content in giving consent. If you do not feel content you've got your biggest sign and signal that something is not right. When a so-called internal examination and breast check was performed on me before my planned eye operation, my consent was not sought. I felt degraded, violated and stripped of any dignity. I am also left with a number of questions; could this still happen within a hospital setting in Ireland today? Do we have appropriate procedures and training in place that could prevent or at least greatly reduce the risk of this happening today?

I have included an excerpt from a 2019 article in The Irish Times; **Ireland, 1984: A year of fierce debates and 'mounting evils'** by Rosita Boland. I ask you to look at the prevailing attitudes and mindset of that year, 1984, and ask you to consider how it may compare with the Ireland that we find ourselves in today.

I am drawn to this quote in the article from historian and Professor of Modern History at UCD, Diarmaid Ferriter;

'Sometimes I think the word misogyny is over-used, but it is difficult to find another word when you think of 1984, because of the level of hostility towards women and the focus on retribution.'

-Diarmuid Ferriter

Ireland, 1984: A year of fierce debates and 'mounting evils'

By Rosita Boland

First Published in The Irish Times July 7, 2019

Article excerpt printed with kind permission of ©The Irish Times

THE YEAR 1984 BECAME NOTORIOUS FOR A NUMBER OF STORIES INVOLVING WOMEN, PREGNANCY OUTSIDE MARRIAGE, AND THEIR TREATMENT BY SOCIETY, CHURCH AND STATE. THE IMPACT OF THESE STORIES WOULD RESONATE FOR DECADES.

That year, 15-year-old Ann Lovett died after giving birth to a stillborn son at a grotto in Granard, Co Longford; a full-term pregnancy that appeared to have gone unnoticed by all who knew her.

Teacher Eileen Flynn twice lost her appeal of unfair dismissal against the Holy Faith Convent in New Ross, Co Wexford. She had been living with a married man, and had had a baby with him. Her private life was deemed by her employers, the Holy Faith nuns, to be lacking in the Catholic standards expected of their teachers.

Two dead babies were found in Co Kerry; one at Cahersiveen and one at Abbeydorney. Joanne Hayes, who already had one child with a married man and was the mother of one of the dead babies, became the focus of a tribunal of inquiry in relation to both babies.

In recent weeks we heard the full story of garda Majella Moynihan, who in 1984 was unmarried and gave birth to a son she had had by a fellow unmarried garda recruit. She subsequently came under pressure to give the child up for adoption, and the following year was charged with alleged breaches of Garda regulations.

The story was first reported by Mary Maher in The Irish Times in February 1985. The garda remained unnamed throughout The Irish Times's coverage of the case at the time. In recent weeks, almost 35 years later, her full story came to light in an RTÉ Radio documentary.*

"Sometimes I think the word misogyny is over-used, but it is difficult to find another word when you think of 1984, because of the level of hostility towards women and the focus on retribution," says historian Diarmaid Ferriter. "Not everything in the determination to do women down went unchallenged."

Ferriter sees the beginnings of changes in attitude towards church and state dating from that time. "Joanne Hayes was meant to be a fallen woman, but there was public sympathy and support for her, because there was disgust at the way she was treated."

"Fundamentally, 1984 was so difficult for women to begin with, with the failure of the abortion referendum in 1983," says feminist and former academic, Ailbhe Symth. "We barely had time to pick ourselves up when Ann Lovett died. A lot of us knew that that dark underbelly was in Ireland, so while deeply sad, we knew these terrible things were happening."

According to the Oxford Dictionary misogyny means dislike of, contempt for, or ingrained prejudice against women or girls. I went back to look at 1984 because it was important to me to get a sense and feeling of that time and how things might have been dealt with, the above named article spoke for itself.

It's incredible to read it and to get somewhat of an understanding of the mind-set then. It's frightening to me actually that I have no recollection of the above but then I was only a 15 year-old. Reading this article gives me a sense that I would have had no opportunity to get the truth at that time.

Looking at old newspapers from 1984 is like looking at another world, another space in time – a place of deafening silence.

In getting support from the organisation Dignity4Patients I know I am one of many and that I deserve, as they do, to be treated with dignity and respect.

In learning lessons from this I choose to break my silence and be a beacon and shine a light on my own difficult and dark experience. I have found my own inner power and I hope that this book can help you to find yours too, no matter your age or how long ago something might have happened that interrupted and interfered with your life.

Jacqui aged around 3 years and 4 years

Chapter Two

This is only part of my story

I was sexually assaulted, at 15 years of age, by a man that I thought was a Doctor within a hospital.

I had fallen down the steep set of stairs in my Aunts house as a young child of around 3 years old, in 1972. The impact of hitting the front door at the bottom of the stairs caused a massive black bump that came out on my forehead. But as the weeks passed my Mum started to notice that my left eye was rolling in towards my nose, it was more obvious when I was tired that there was something wrong. So after much consideration and observation she decided to take me to our local Optician to get my left eye checked. Unfortunately, as a consequence of the fall on that day and the impact of hitting the front door head on had most likely loosened the muscles in the back of my left eye and it had left me with a cast or squint.

The Optician decided to give me glasses to wear, as opposed to an eye patch, to try and straighten the eye. In the years that followed wearing glasses constantly would permanently effect my overall sight but didn't cure the squint. For those of you who may not remember, glasses back then in the 1970's and 80's were not cool. Most certainly they were not a fashion accessory and for many of us who had to wear them all the time, our standard issue children's glasses were often used as a reason to make fun of us. Names such as four-eyes were frequently used. As if that wasn't confidence knocking enough, I then had to wear what I can best describe as the Nana Mouskouri style glasses, for those of you old enough to remember her she was a singer, you'll have an idea of what that style looked like and then I went on to wear what I call the snooker player Dennis Taylor styles ones - big bottle tops. So it's of no surprise that when I was given an opportunity to get rid of them through a hospital operation and as a self-conscious teenager that I jumped at the opportunity.

What actually happened was that in January 1984 as I was coming up to my 15th birthday my Mum asked me if I wanted a bike for my birthday, but I said, no. I clearly remember saying to her that all I really wanted was my eye fixed and my glasses gone. I was at an age where I was so self-conscious and I thought getting my eye fixed would help.

Honouring my request my Mum organised for me to go to see an eye specialist and in the coming months we went to see him privately in his practice. I always remember so vividly the numerous photos of children and teenagers in his practice room showing their before and after photos of crossed and then perfectly straight eyes. The eye specialist agreed to operate! The date of 23rd October 1984 was set for me to be admitted to hospital for an eye operation to straighten the squint in my eye.

I don't remember much about the eye specialist, just all those photos of happy looking children with straight eyes that he proudly displayed in is consulting rooms. I don't remember how long I had to wait only that finally, finally I thought I would have perfectly straight eyes and no glasses!

Finally the wait was over and on the Wednesday morning of 23rd October 1984 I took the bus to the hospital with my Mum. I was a very innocent 15 year-old and I had never been separated much from my Mum before – apart from school and had never spent a night away from home. I was very naïve about a world that I hadn't yet stepped into. So that day was huge for me, I was soon going to find myself on my own with no visitors and really no way of contact as this was pre-mobile phones. In fact it was before even household phones for the vast majority of us. I knew that I was facing an eye operation and that my eye would be taken out and repositioned back in the socket. As the bus trundled along I felt sick and anxious in my stomach.

I know now that this was at a time when there was very little or no policy or procedures for chaperoning or how to support a minor in hospital. I have sought that information for that period of time and unfortunately the hospital couldn't provide it. They could find nothing official.

I arrived at the hospital around 11am on that Wednesday morning. I know I was admitted at the reception and met some of the eye team. My Mum and I were then shown down to the hospital room that I would stay in, I clearly remember the room as being an apple green colour that seems to be a hospital special issue.

It was a semi private room and there were just two beds, my bed was nearest the door. The windows were like the ones you would see in old convents or old schools - high sills with long, tall windows. Not long after that another patient of a similar age to me was brought into the room and she stayed in the bed nearest the window, from my memory she was in for an operation that I remember thinking it was unusual as, in my view, she was far too young to have that issue at her age. My Mum wasn't allowed to stay long and left saying she would see me on the Friday. So I found myself having to be all grown up and I chatted to the girl in the bed beside me, she was lovely and we got on very well.

After a couple of hours and after lunchtime I am sitting on the bed in my hospital gown when a man that I believe to be a doctor fills the entrance at the door of our room. He is dressed in a white gown, the button up white-coat style worn by doctors. He has dark hair and is standing around 5' 8. He tells me, as he continues standing at the door that he is here to do an examination on me.

I thought he was there to check my eye. So I said okay and he proceeded to walk towards the bed and pulled the curtains around my bed. He said that he was there to perform an internal examination and he pointed down to my genital area. This felt so wrong to me. I did challenge him and asked why - I do remember clearly saying to him then, 'what has down there got to do with my eyes or my operation?'

He said in a cold insistent manner, 'It has to be done.'

He asked me to lie down and then proceeded to sexually assault me. For the next few moments I don't know where my head went, I know my eyes went up to the white ceiling and the fluorescent lights. I was having some awful experience. He then proceeded to slide his hands up onto my breasts. Yet it's only in recent years that I've really realised the significance of both of these happening at the same time. So these few moments left me feeling degraded, ashamed and opened a void.

When he finished, I remember that he didn't fill in any paperwork and to be honest with you I made very little eye contact with him, I couldn't wait for him to leave. He then drew the curtains back and he proceeded to the girl in the bed beside me, he pulled the curtains around her. When he finally left I said to her what had been done to me and she said the same had been done to her.

Now here it gets really very confusing and messy. I understand now that I was in shock. The day passed in a blur and the next thing I remember was the nurse coming to give me a sedative that night to prepare me for my operation the next morning. I didn't say anything to this nurse, a female nurse. I was not able to speak or tell her what had happened and no-one noticed that something was wrong, that I seemed numb or asked me if I was okay.

The next morning I was taken down to theatre where I had my operation. I was recovering from the anaesthetic for most of the day and don't remember anything until around 9 pm on the Thursday evening when the female nurse arrived in to give me some tea and toast. I slept all that night.

The eye team came in to check on me on the Friday morning and told me that they were happy with how the operation had gone and that in the eye specialist's view it was a success. Around lunchtime I was discharged and got the bus home.

And it was on the bus home that I first got the sense initially that well sure it must've been part of the admittance procedures. But I just knew that it wasn't. This was the start of a lifelong question that would continue to seek an answer. The biggest difficulty I was having was that I had been prepared to deal with an eye operation and yet I had found myself being personally violated. And I felt violated, degraded, demeaned and stripped of any dignity. I could not have told you this back then. These words were not in my vocabulary then, I couldn't have named it and how I was feeling in such terms, this is me the 51-year-old woman now advocating for the 15-year-old child that couldn't speak for herself.

When I finally arrived home off the bus a couple of hours later my Mum was thrilled to see me. She looked at the big white eye pack dressing. I was delighted to be home, I was a real home bird and I did mention to Mum what had happened. I asked her why would it have happened and why would I have not been told in advance so that I could have prepared myself in some way or another? Some part of me may have wanted it to have been official in some way.

Today I sense that there was some attitude in the 1980's that hospitals and doctors and people in authority were official and to be trusted and that if something happened within a hospital then it was meant to happen.

I now on reflection realise that I quickly fell into a deep depression as I struggled to cope. I spent much of the following days and months just sitting in the front room of our house. It was a small dark room and furnished in browns and creams that were so popular at the time. I would sit on the brown and cream tartan check chair between the window and the fireplace. I rarely remembered to turn on a light. I chose this room instead of the bustling family room next to it with its roaring fire and access to the kitchen. My experience of it then is in complete contrast to how I used the room before the sexual assault just days before. I had so many wonderful times in that room up until then, kids from the street were constantly in and we played Grease and Xanadu in the front room with our headphones on. I remember fun and laughter and my Mum popping in and feeding us sausages & chips, eggs & chips or bean & chips. They were good chips!

After I was assaulted I just found myself in a dark hole, that's the best way I can describe it, just sitting silent in a dark hole. My Mum was worried about me. I felt really sad, I wasn't talking and I felt lost. I just remember spending most of my days sitting, sitting, sitting, sitting and sitting! I remember her often coming into the room to check on me and her trying to reassure me by saying to me; 'you know Jacqui that's a side-effect of the anaesthesia and it will eventually pass.'

But I know now that in that period I was actually doing a lot of inner processing to help me to go forward and to eventually bring me to where I am today.

So, I am recognising that this is only part of my story, it does not define me, and yet if by sharing it and shining a light on some dark recesses of my mind and the event helps or allows someone else to feel inspired, healed and empowered then this book will do what it is intended to do.

Soul Searching

I have done a lot of soul searching as to whether I would share these pages because I know that when they leave me and my story goes outside of the safety of these pages it could take on a complete life of its own.

I suppose the question I have had to ask myself has been; what is the purpose of my sharing such information and is it mine to keep? I have kept most parts of my soul to myself but I have sensed throughout the writing process that this part of my story is not mine to keep. Should this information be kept from public view? One might say keep it to yourself for your own privacy reasons. If I do that I feel that I then deny the truth of what happened to me in that hospital coming out.

Writing this I am approaching the 36th anniversary of an event that happened to me and that I want to share with you. It's incredible to think that it is within my writings and my sharing of my story that I am bringing to a closure and letting go of all the loneliness, shame, emptiness and a deep feeling of never being good enough, believing I was stupid and that belief that what happened to me didn't matter.

Amazing what time and space allows and permits especially over the past few months and in the middle of a global pandemic. A recent letter from the hospital has confirmed that such an examination as I alleged that I had undergone should not have been performed on me. Since then I have been fast and furious when it comes to writing these pages, it's difficult to explain but it just seems they just appear and come from nowhere accompanied by my 15 year-old self that was affected by this.

So as I'm sitting and walking around my kitchen; reflecting, writing and putting the pieces of my book, my personal journal and record of my thoughts and emotions of this experiences in their purest form, uncensored and raw by letting the words spill out onto the page. I am writing, writing, writing once again to get rid of it and what I've learned to date together with the tools I've used to overcome it. I now know without any doubt that I must share it with you. I notice that the more I write the lighter and more free I feel.

The following can be read in any order you choose or you can follow how I've set it out. It is my intention that by sharing my writings that someone will find hope and empowering ways to overcome their own challenges. It is my intention to encourage others to have their own open conversations about their life experiences in the knowing and comfort that their experiences are valuable to someone else's healing. In writing my story I have freed myself from the silence, shame, secrecy and the darkness that this event brought to me and leave it no space to hide.

I now give all these feelings, thoughts and emotions back to their owner because they don't belong to me they belong to the individual who came in and interrupted my life path and journey.

Going Home.

With each word and page I write I know that I am going home.

Author's Soul Painting, 2020

Embracing the 15 year-old self

Note to self: Thank you Jacqui, thank you so much for your courage and bravery on that day.

Thank you for never doubting yourself. You knew it was wrong. Your strength is incredible to stick to that knowing even though everyone around you didn't. You are indeed amazing and it is an honour to be part of you.

It's great that I am now in a place of strength and power to embrace you and take your hand and we'll walk the rest of this road, our journey together. I will take care of you, it's time to give that baggage back that we've carried for him. Back to him as it doesn't and didn't belong here.

Together we will create a list of things to go into the bag and make sure that as we give it back we leave nothing behind that belongs to him.

Even as we write this, myself and my 15 year-old self, there is huge resistance because we are giving back something that we have carried for over 35 years.

The giving back will lighten our load and give room for many wonderful things to arrive in its place.

Going Home.

With each word and page I write I know that I am going home.

Hold your own

Hold onto that part of you

that you know to be true.

Hold your own

Hold onto the part of you

that wants you to be whatever you desire.

Hold your own

Hold tight, get ready for the greatest battle

that you will ever face, the battle of You!

Hold your own!

- Jacqui Taaffe

Chapter Three

Absolute Deep Knowing

Confirming what I always knew, the letter arrived on a morning in June 2020, clearly stating what I had asked for in clear, concise English. I had written to the Hospital to ask whether it was indeed part of my admittance process to have such an internal examination. The current Clinical Director of the Hospital wrote back to me to say that an alleged internal examination, presuming I meant a vaginal examination as I had not specified, is not a routine part of an admission for eye surgery and that they would not have expected such an alleged examination to have been carried out unless there were clear instructions and clinical reasons in my medical notes to do such an examination. They further confirmed that this was not part of the admittance process to hospital for an eye operation, then or now.

When I first saw this in black and white writing – I didn't really know how to feel. I had a new sense of relief and sadness that for the very first time someone else other than me is saying that this should not have occurred. I also felt completely exhausted and for the next 48 hours I just had to be nice to myself and not force anything to come to the page.

As I looked back and reflected, the fact is that I kept much of this part of my story to myself and mostly carried it alone. I don't want pity when I write that, I'm just expressing the fact that I really was the only one who knew and questioned the actions of the man who assaulted me and the fact that that man may have been, or just appeared to be, a doctor. There was within me a fear and I think a genuine assumption that if I told anyone that they would presume or assert that this was an official examination – that the only one with the difficulty and questions was me and would be me.

I knew, I knew, I knew it was wrong and my inner essence has always been there for me. Somehow at my core I have protected myself and kept certain awareness away from myself until I was ready and in a good and powerful place to process this. Now that I am ready it's like a flood, an out-pouring of stuff, information and new awareness comes to me daily. The more I write and the more I allow and trust my experiences the more I remember and the more that there is to resolve.

When the doubt is gone the cold reality of the facts hit me like a steam train for the immediate days and weeks to follow.

Reading the confirmation that an internal examination was not part of my admission to hospital has now completely removed any seed of doubt that I had. Now I find myself without my protection cushion which I would have used quite often to say to myself – well maybe it was okay and official. Even though I was 99.99% sure it wasn't. Maybe the doubt helped me to cope, because when you remove doubt, well then all I am left with is the fact that it was wrong and that new understanding and letting go of the doubt is a strange one to describe.

The doubt, and maybe it was the grey area that doubt allowed, created space for it to sit silently. Now that the doubt is gone, the space in which it sat is no more. It now sits in a space that's visible to me that it was wrong, the examination should never have happened.

What do I do now without doubt, knowing for sure what was done was wrong?

Going forward without doubt is strange. Doubt for me was definitely a fall back and a mental crutch allowing and enabling me to live my life to this point. I always knew without a doubt that at my very core and being, it was wrong. But at a human level - doubt was sown and in a constructive way was my coping mechanism that allowed and enabled me to cope and manage this event. The removal of any doubt now strengthens my resolve to allow myself to heal.

I really respect that the hospital have reacted and responded in an understanding way for me in 2020. For years this simply was hidden from sight and left for me to carry alone. But what I have realised is that this is not mine to carry and it is not mine to hide. There is absolutely no shame in sharing this with others because its power, or the person who did this, only remains in power if it is kept hidden. It's incredible to think that this could happen and really only a handful of people knew. It was never really discussed nor even checked out. I must have completely shut down and pushed down all those emotions to move on and live my life. I can't believe that the next person to talk to me in the hospital was a female nurse and I never said about the internal examination. It's incredible what the mind does.

But I know that I have now got the answer for my 15 year-old self. I am proud that I got that for her. The truth. She didn't deserve or ask for any of that, right now I want to embrace and love that 15 year-old girl who always knew that it was wrong.

'Calling them out - Seeds of doubt - shining a light so bright on them,

they grow into something new empowering and inspiring.'

Low

The days that have followed my receiving the confirmation that the internal examination was not part of the admittance process to hospital for an eye operation for my teenage self, has been very strange and my mood very low and flat.

I don't like that feeling but I know that I have to go with it and allow it the space that it deserves. As the events never were given space – only in the deep recesses of my mind.

It was barely ever discussed or shared by me, so it needs space to be seen in the light of day. Unseen and unheard for years it remained only in my mind's eye.

I really am finding this difficult to write, the effort and energy of it is all consuming. To think that such an event can hide itself in the mind of that child and the confusion that reigned for her. Her knowing, my knowing, that at the very core or essence of her this was wrong and yet the silence that came after it was a deafening silence. It's incredible – I still cannot fathom at times how this could have occurred. You know the confirmation from the hospital was good to get but personally it didn't change anything for me, because I always knew. But when you don't speak about it and no-one else speaks about such experiences, it becomes a subject best avoided.

Maybe best avoided for my welfare and because it's an awkward subject. But the silence and avoidance I took ownership of was to help me through the years. Not avoiding it any longer over the past 10 years and now to be talking about it with a few others is somewhat tough and emotionally draining. But I have no doubt I will rise stronger than ever. It's just surrounded with sadness – sadness for time and innocence that was lost. This writing and these pages are taking me to a conclusion and I must trust in the process.

Going Home.

With each word and page I write I know that I am going home.

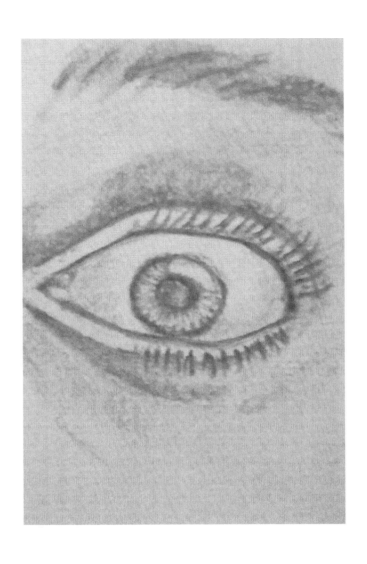

Illustration by Cian Lounds

Chapter Four

Shame

How powerful silence can be. For me, my silence led to an abiding and murky sense of shame and forced my minds-eye to find ways to cope with something I could not yet look at and even as I did could only partially see within the swamp of my emotions and the darkness of a sexual assault.

On reflection, in my view, silence can be used in both an empowering or disempowering and an approving or disapproving and disarming way. For almost all of the times and opportunities I had to speak about the event and ask questions – I didn't. I instinctively knew that I couldn't go there. So I didn't go there. It was a deep knowing I had and still have today. Over the years I most definitely suppressed the need to ask any questions. I shelved the event in some small and silent compartment or corridor in my mind. I didn't want to upset those I loved most, I didn't want to be judged or shamed, I didn't want to speak or see or hear the evil that was done to me.

A huge void appeared in my life in late 2010 when I became an orphan. As a consequence of the role of daughter ceasing I found myself having a huge vacuum where time and space were created. Now as I reflect and look back this was the beginning of a ten year journey that has led to the creation of this book. In 2013 I had what I thought was going to be an official meeting with Bernadette Sullivan who had been fundamental in setting up a local organisation called Dignity4Patients and was seeking approval of secondment of staff to their organisation. This turned out to be a significant moment in my life and a meeting that I believe was really meant to be.

Bernadette Sullivan sat in my office describing the aims and objectives of Dignity4Patients to support people who have undergone inappropriate medical examinations in hospitals across Ireland.

As she talked about the work they did to support patients I saw myself in what she was describing.

Most importantly as she spoke it created a space and allowed me to open a door metaphorically to say to her, 'you know I had one of them.' That was the first time in decades I had said it out loud, I had broken the silence.

I contacted her a few weeks later privately and became a client of Dignity4Patients. It was the start of me beginning to take small steps to break that silence many times over and over again through my actions, words and writings. It was the start of an empowering journey for me. I want to share the invaluable support that I have received from Bernadette and Dignity4Patients as I believe that their service has been underestimated and undervalued. It was hugely beneficial for me to have Bernadette walk in to my office that day and I don't know when I would have been given an opportunity ever to verbalise that I had such an inappropriate medical examination done to me. It was only for Bernadette talking about the need to create awareness and the support services provided by Dignity4Patients that day that I was able to step forward and start the process and they walked with me through each of the phases including; getting my medical records, making the Garda statements and writing to the hospital to achieve clarity. They were always at the end of the phone to support me, to listen and just be there with me as I have gone through this journey and most importantly they believed me.

My right to choose whether or not I wanted that so-called internal examination was taken from me on that day. My right to choose how I now see it and deal with it is mine. I can choose to stay low and flat and numb or I can choose to look at what I might take from this to strengthen my resolve and for my own respect and dignity.

The shame is like a double-edged sword. On one side all the negative, grimy stuff which cannot be changed, it's the residue of what happened. My only power now is to choose not to give it any attention, thoughts and feelings. If I don't give the event any more attention I believe in time the memories will further fade. As a life-coach and with the tools that I have learned, I know this, I know that I can trust and have faith.

Trust

Trust for me is a heart led emotion, in other words it doesn't come from a thought I have. It comes from a feeling, a deep sense of knowing that something is okay or it's the right thing to do. Knowing, and in particular in my case, that regardless of how the individual showed up and how the circumstances may have appeared I knew and trusted at the very core of my being that the event, the sexual assault, was wrong.

Shame is heavy and cumbersome and in my view a bag of thoughts, beliefs and emotions that I took ownership of that day and I now know they were never mine to keep.

Why should I feel shame for the actions and behaviours of someone else?

What shameful act did I do? None, I have done nothing.

I now know that I didn't keep shame willingly, shame crawled or seeped in through the openings it found whilst I was confused and suffocating in a swamp of my thoughts and emotions that day and it didn't leave.

Shame made me believe I had something to hide, that I had something to be ashamed of. And then its friend silence came along.

My power lies in me calling out that shame and breaking the silence around it.

TRUST

Place yourself In The gentle hands of "TRUST"!
In the knowing' that you are exactly where you
are meant to be "right now".

Jacqui Taaffe
www.jacquitaaffe.com

x

63

SHAME - **S**ecretly **H**iding **A**ll **M**y **E**motions

Secretly hiding all my emotions from whom and for what purpose? Too difficult for me to handle. Emotions like feeling a dirty-filthy being. Shame because it happened to me. Shame for some bizarre reasons that I took the shame on – but it wasn't mine to take in the first place.

Shame didn't belong to me. It belongs to him.

Letting go of the shame, once again giving it back to him to carry, not me. Freeing me up, allowing space for my essence and core and knowing – to be me. With shame comes deep feelings of not being good enough. Being treated like a piece of meat.

Going Home.

With each word and page I write I know that I am going home.

LISTEN

LISTEN - How many great ideas, cures, inventions and dreams are lost as a consequence of not listening to our own incredible voice?

LISTEN - What is it within the human condition that we often give more value and attention to the ideas and opinions of others rather than to our own?

LISTEN - Ask yourself? What's that about?

LISTEN - your ideas and dreams have a purpose.

LISTEN - Listen closely to them and act upon them.

LISTEN - To deny them is to deny and not listen to the very purpose and callings of your soul.

-   Jacqui Taaffe

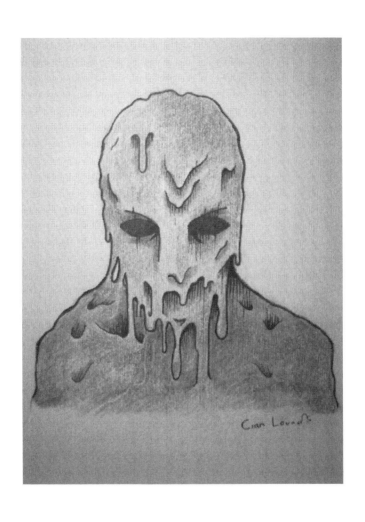

The Swamp-like Figure

But first let's look into the swamp…Here's the best way I can describe how what happened to me manifested and affected me. Awareness of the following descriptions comes from over a decade of self-coaching, learning about myself plus a little counselling. With that chance meeting with Bernadette Sullivan of Dignity4Patients and being able to voice what had happened to me, to someone who understood, I began to experience a relentless magnetic pull from my essence or inner being to unearth the truth. And I listened. And I have listened to many people talk about feelings of shame or guilt but for me it also manifested in a mental image and a feeling on my chest. For me, the feeling is heavy, like a massive weight which sits on the middle of my breast bone, pushing down. So heavy that at times my breathing can become laboured so I have to inhale and exhale deeply to try and lift that weight. I cannot stress enough the physical effects of this emotional pressure on my chest. I would become frightened and fatigued as I struggled to breathe.

What it looks like to me in my mind's eye is a dark presence, it can or wants to domineer or dominate my space. I see a dark, green-black, swamp-like and over-bearing presence. It's sticky and gritty. It's not nice. I don't like it. It stands over me invading my personal space and suffocating me. I want it to move away from me.

For years I carried that feeling with me everywhere. It was an almost constant presence, this swamp-like figure as it has come to be known by me. It made me retreat from numerous opportunities and situations in my life. By that I mean I would be so frightened by this domineering and ominous presence that I would experience problems with my breathing which became laboured and heavy and overwhelming. I was always aware of that thought, 'you are not good enough, and you don't matter.' So even though others may have perceived a very confident me, my self-worth and love of me was zero. It's by studying, learning and listening to my essence that I have been able to learn to trust and finally believe that I am indeed much greater than that one event.

As I am writing this some 37 years later, I can hear in my head; 'I don't like it! I don't like it!' I think that it is my 15 year-old self; 'I don't like it! I don't like this!'

I have another sense that this domineering, imposing figure doesn't like me talking to anyone else about it because when I do I have a sense that I am weakening its hold on me. 'He' doesn't like to be seen. He wants to keep hidden in the dark swamp that I created for him. He doesn't want others to know what he did. The more I write about what happened, the more that domineering presence is telling me that he's fe***n rightly annoyed with me. 'Who do I think I am?' and that, 'no-one cares what happened to me.' This noise, these words are all my self-talk coming up really strong and showing themselves.

The self-loathing contained in this self-talk is not good, yet after a decade of working on myself and as I am able to step back from the words, I hear:

'Who give a F***'

'Who cares?'

'Who do you think you are?'

'Sure it only happened to you once, what's your problem?'

He really doesn't like to be seen.

This swamp-like presence is the method my 15-year-old self used as a way to cope and go on in this world. I told no-one because I assumed no-one would have a solution, actually no-one would know what to do about it. No-one would know how to handle the child. That's how I felt. No-one would know what to say or do. So, it simply wasn't discussed- and sure if I ignore something long enough maybe it will go away or resolve itself? That was my child's thinking.

The problem is that it left me as a 15-year-old child to attempt to resolve things on my own. I just felt very alone. Like the child who cried help but no-one came. It's incredible that I am here now, an adult woman advocating for my 15 year-old self and sharing with you the reader my reflections and learnings in the hope that if you see something within these pages that resonates with you that it may help you too. I now choose to step out of my feelings of shame and step up to share my story as a beacon of light.

I now realise that in writing this book that the time is right NOW and how inspiring, healing and empowering it has been to go through this process to write, journal, create images and write poems.

I can't stress enough the benefit of the writing and reflection process and how it has helped me to NOW share my story, to break the silence, to free myself from shame and to stand into my power. The time is NOW.

Thoughts on powerlessness:

My sense of being powerless crept up on me quite quickly. I didn't see it coming I just found myself in it in a situation that I could not stop. Feeling stunned and numb.

Feeling dirty left me feeling like a piece of meat which could be used or discarded without any consequences.

Overwhelmed - suffocating, suffocating and suffocating.

Confusion - like a rabbit caught in headlights, seeds of doubt, questioning oneself - did I imagine it?

Stupid – I was just not clever enough to stop it.

Doubtful - questioning myself. Doubt was also a great coping strategy for me. Once I had doubt I could tell myself in the most difficult moments then maybe what happened was official and was meant to have happened. Rather than the harsh reality of being assaulted.

*Ignoran*t - to the ways of the world and my rights at that time. But I would say that it was utter innocence.

Bullied & cornered - helpless no space to move.

Can't Breathe - this is still with me, I have laboured breathing in moments of reflection and anxiety.

Can't escape - I couldn't escape so the strategy was to get it over with and get him gone.

Feeling it didn't matter - because this event literally went undetected, unnoticed, not discussed. It left me further conflicted with the feelings of violation that I felt that day never mind the confusion of someone presenting in an official capacity, they may or may not have been a Doctor, in order to assault me.

Having no voice, silence - I was so compliant which is incredible to think that this can happen to someone and the torrent of confusion that proceeds from such an assault is so overwhelming and powerful that it silenced me.

Note for You

For you, who like me, knows that what was done to you was wrong, you keep going and keep believing in yourself. There is nobody better than you to decide. You know already what to do.

Only that I, without question, trusted the very core of my being – my very intuitive instincts that spoke to me and told me you are right, that was wrong. I think I would have always had a yearning or space in me that needed to be embraced and loved.

So whatever your circumstances are and no matter what others might say to you. Trust that your very core and essence will be here for you when you are ready to trust it and allow it to guide you.

I am of the view that mine took care of what happened to me until I was ready to look at it and begin the process of dismantling it in my mind. Up to now I continue to gain new awareness around the events that day and I can only trust that my time was right to see it now. I believe that I am where I am meant to be right now and this allows me both to accept and be kind to myself along this journey home to me.

Going Home.

With each word and page I write I know that I am going home.

I

The I

A knowing,

A deep knowing,

Another way of seeing

As opposed to what the naked eyes see

The 'I' knows, feels,

Sees at a deeper more profound level.

Trust in that 'I' that deep knowing part of you!

The 'Eyes' are 'the windows to the soul'

But the 'I' is the doorway to the true self!

- Jacqui Taaffe

Illustration by Cian Lounds

Chapter Five

I Eye

I wake with a jolt from a recurring nightmare and once again I see my left eye, in grayscale, mostly black. The eye widens and I feel that same suffocating fear as a scalpel cuts through it and black blood oozes from the eye, which I know is my eye.

As I had tried to live with my feelings of deep shame over many years, my mind struggled to cope with the knowing. The more I tried to look away, the more my mind distorted the picture until this recurring and numbing scene established itself becoming visible in my dreams and most mornings when I first woke up there it would be, visible and sickening. Whatever you choose to call it. My soul or knowing sees what the human eye can't see. The I that just wakened sees the truth that I had been violated;

before life comes along and disturbs it into many different versions or imposes judgement and fear of others opinion.

Yes the event happened but I am not part of it and I played no part in it – I just lay there silently as my choice had been removed. So I lay silently until the actions of him and the events of that moment passed. Lying in the silence wishing the minutes to pass quickly.

I felt terror when it first started to happen in my teenage years. I felt so frightened. For anyone who has frightening and graphic visions like this will understand when I say that it makes you concerned for yourself. I struggled with thoughts that I might be going crazy, might lose my mind but really it just added to my feelings of being different and I never shared it or discussed it with anyone.

At some point this vision stopped happening daily or even frequently. Over time I was able to deconstruct it and compartmentalise it until I had locked it away so tight that I forgot about it. It was only in the writing of this book and at a time when I had decided that I would share my story that the vision returned. It was a shock to my system. A reminder I guess, certainly a reminder for me. A shock in that in seeing it again I felt that same suffocating heaviness and fear. All that I have learned helped me to go within and detach from the images. By detaching I mean being able to look at the vision but quickly and deliberately step out of the feelings of fear and suffocation.

And yet with the resurfacing of this eye image and the scalpel and the thick black blood I was stopped in my tracks. I felt what many would call triggered and I felt tired and confused for a few days. So again within I went and this is what I found.

I find within that 15 year-old self that knew absolutely that what was done was wrong and it's her relentless strength and determination for recognition that has brought me to writing these words for her. To tell her I am listening and that I am doing my best to get that acknowledgment for her. To share our journey of realisations and strategies that have empowered and enabled us.

As I detach and see the eye image more clearly I keep thinking what can that eye see as opposed to what the real eye can see? It took me some 35 years to seek external validation and finally fully accept that the sexual assault was definitely not an internal examination. Further it was also not official as I now know for sure that it would not have been part of any admittance process for an eye operation nor is it officially recorded anywhere in my hospital files. But I didn't see these events looking through the lens of just a pair of eyes. I observed those events from a greater or more intuitive place. It was this place that confronted me every morning with this graphic vision of my left eye being sliced open.

This was that part of me that is capable of seeing things from a much bigger and wiser perspective – I saw and felt the negative response and emotions in my heart, head and soul had that day. So even though to the naked eye things could look okay or be explained away possibly, to the inner eye, that truly sees things as they are it saw something quite dark and sinister. So seeing is not believing, seeing is a lot more than just that, it's an inner instinct to see things as they really are. I suppose what I am trying to explain or express is – the I that truly sees is not visible to the human eyes. My I, when I go within I see way beyond what the human eye sees.

The eye, The I

The knowing, that deep knowing

is another level of seeing

as opposed to what's seen by the naked eye.

Trust in that deep knowing part of you!

The eyes are 'the windows to the soul'

But the I is the doorway to the true self!

- Jacqui Taaffe

INSPIRE HEAL EMPOWER

She had no choice
but be "Fierce"
So she was
Until she knew
she was ready'
To give up
"Fierce" for "Love"

Jacqui Taaffe

"Lights The Way"

84

Who Am I?

To ask questions.

To want answers.

To shine a light on an event rarely spoken of.

To want recognition and acknowledgment for the wrong done to me as a child.

To right the wrongs through my writings and words of these pages.

To want freedom from those events that day.

To want freedom to rise above those negative thoughts and feelings that I carried.

To want transparency & truth.

I am!

I am the 15 year-old who is entitled to answers to her questions.

I am the 15 year-old who will shine a light so bright on this event for myself.

I am the 15 year-old today who has the right to say no and has the right to give my 100% consent to any and all examinations that I have.

I am the 15 year-old who now can articulate what I couldn't back then.

I am the child who never let go of the empowering belief that those actions were wrong on that day.

I Am Truth!

I Am Going Home To My Truth!

- Jacqui Taaffe, August 2020

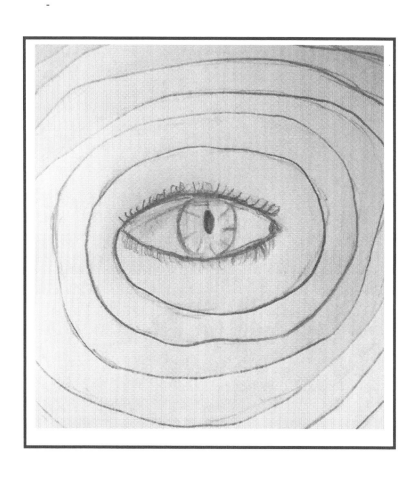

Illustration by Kara Taaffe

Chapter Six

Justice and Judgement

In facing the event and the transgression in my life I have had to look at the concept of Justice and what that means for me. The Oxford dictionary gives one definition of Justice as just behaviour or treatment. It is that quality of genuine respect for people. With this understanding I feel that I am just in my resolve to look at and share my experience of sexual assault and its impact on me. That I have been justified in my hurt and anger that this event happened to me.

It took me many years to seek clarity on the actual events of that day and an explanation of what happened and yet longer to consider my legislative rights. I have been forced to consider if Justice in my case would have any place in a Court of Law.

I followed the law as far as I felt was reasonable for me. I made a statement to the Gardaí in 2014 giving full details of the event, my so-called internal examination and so-called breast examination. It was a Garda who attended my home to take my statement was the first person to recognise the language that I was using. Up to that point I had always referred to the event as a so-called internal examination or an inappropriate medical examination. The Garda was the first person to really ask me did I fully understand what I was alleging, he asked; 'do you really understand the seriousness of what you are saying and that you are alleging that you were sexually assaulted?'

That stopped me, the words stopped me that was the first time I would be able to call it for what it was - a sexual assault rather than hide behind the beautiful labelling that I had assigned it as an inappropriate medical examination. I am grateful to that Gardaí for naming it and for him listening to my experience and for taking my written statement.

In giving my written statement to the Garda I do not think that I ever expected a legal outcome. I was now facing the past and taking every step that was required by my 15 year-old self. That included, finally, after some 30 years filing a statement with the Gardaí. I let go of any fear of being judged on that day as I finally and officially told my story to someone who could potentially hold the man that assaulted me to account.

And yet, I knew somehow that this may not be possible and that he may never be found. I presumed that he would be in mid-50's at that point. On the day that I filed my written statement I was still using doubt as part of my coping tools, the doubt allowed me to tell myself that the event may have been an official examination and now I could hand it over to those with the legislative power to fully investigate. I had let go of my fear of being judged and had allowed myself to seek justice.

What I have found over the past six years is that, in letting go of my own fear of being judged, the more I am able to be vulnerable, the more I write, the more that I share my vulnerabilities, the more free and empowered I feel. The letting go of the protection mode that I no longer need has enabled me to see that it only served a purpose of getting me and my mental wellness to a point where I can and could let it go, give it up and give it back! I've included a poem called, 'Please Hear What I'm Not Saying' because it so resonates with me:

Please Hear What I'm Not Saying

Don't be fooled by me.
Don't be fooled by the face I wear
for I wear a mask, a thousand masks,
masks that I'm afraid to take off,
and none of them is me.

Pretending is an art that's second nature with me,
but don't be fooled,
for God's sake don't be fooled.
I give you the impression that I'm secure,
that all is sunny and unruffled with me, within as well as
without,
that confidence is my name and coolness my game,
that the water's calm and I'm in command
and that I need no one,
but don't believe me.
My surface may seem smooth but my surface is my mask,
ever-varying and ever-concealing.
Beneath lies no complacence.
Beneath lies confusion, and fear, and aloneness.
But I hide this. I don't want anybody to know it.
I panic at the thought of my weakness exposed.
That's why I frantically create a mask to hide behind,
a nonchalant sophisticated facade,
to help me pretend,
to shield me from the glance that knows.

But such a glance is precisely my salvation, my only hope,
and I know it.
That is, if it's followed by acceptance,
if it's followed by love.
It's the only thing that can liberate me from myself,
from my own self-built prison walls,
from the barriers I so painstakingly erect.
It's the only thing that will assure me
of what I can't assure myself,
that I'm really worth something.
But I don't tell you this. I don't dare to, I'm afraid to.

I'm afraid your glance will not be followed by acceptance,
will not be followed by love.
I'm afraid you'll think less of me,
that you'll laugh, and your laugh would kill me.
I'm afraid that deep-down I'm nothing
and that you will see this and reject me.

So I play my game, my desperate pretending game,
with a facade of assurance without
and a trembling child within.
So begins the glittering but empty parade of masks,
and my life becomes a front.
I idly chatter to you in the suave tones of surface talk.
I tell you everything that's really nothing,
and nothing of what's everything,
of what's crying within me.
So when I'm going through my routine
do not be fooled by what I'm saying.
Please listen carefully and try to hear what I'm not saying,
what I'd like to be able to say,
what for survival I need to say,
but what I can't say.

I don't like hiding.
I don't like playing superficial phony games.
I want to stop playing them.
I want to be genuine and spontaneous and me
but you've got to help me.
You've got to hold out your hand
even when that's the last thing I seem to want.
Only you can wipe away from my eyes
the blank stare of the breathing dead.
Only you can call me into aliveness.
Each time you're kind, and gentle, and encouraging,
each time you try to understand because you really care,
my heart begins to grow wings--
very small wings,
very feeble wings,
but wings!

With your power to touch me into feeling
you can breathe life into me.
I want you to know that.
I want you to know how important you are to me,
how you can be a creator--an honest-to-God creator--
of the person that is me
if you choose to.
You alone can break down the wall behind which I tremble,
you alone can remove my mask,
you alone can release me from my shadow-world of panic,
from my lonely prison,
if you choose to.
Please choose to.

Do not pass me by.
It will not be easy for you.
A long conviction of worthlessness builds strong walls.
The nearer you approach to me the blinder I may strike
back.
It's irrational, but despite what the books say about man
often I am irrational.
I fight against the very thing I cry out for.
But I am told that love is stronger than strong walls
and in this lies my hope.
Please try to beat down those walls
with firm hands but with gentle hands
for a child is very sensitive.

Who am I, you may wonder?
I am someone you know very well.
For I am every man you meet
and I am every woman you meet.

   -   Charles C. Finn
      September 1966

I have now taken off the mask, I don't want to hide and be detached anymore, I want to talk, because in my fear and in the years living in protection mode I didn't understand that I could choose a different way to be. So the mask must be returned to him also – in order that I am completely free to be myself.

Justice may not always be delivered in the sense that I may think of when I think of justice. I know that the Gardaí carried out a full investigation and that the case did not proceed at that time due to lack of evidence. I know that it sits on file. I do not need a Court of Law to pass judgement on my case.

I have found my own inner justice with the fact that it was confirmed that the sexual assault was not an official internal examination and was not part of the admittance process within my hospital files. That information tells me that I'm right and I have championed myself. So justice can come in many forms and I have found that justice is not always without but may be found by going within and coming to a place where you can be at peace and give yourself that justice.

I did my best as a 15 year-old child and now allow that child permission to forgive herself and how she handled it back then. I hug her and tell her now in my mind, 'You did the best with what you knew.' I say to her how strong and resilient she was in the years that followed. How fantastic she is today as she sits by my side as we write this.

With forgiving yourself comes justice, peace of mind, calm and the ability to be whom you want to be.

Who is my Judge and Jury?

As I reflect back on the years of hiding or not disclosing to many what had occurred to me. I see how hard and judgemental I was on myself. The shame that was carried was immense, it alone stopped and overwhelmed me for years. I pre-Judged what others might think of me if I told them my story. I became a Judge and Jury on what I shared.

So I hid it and buried it very deep for many years because I also decided that others would think less of me. It's incredible how the mind works. I lived in self-protection mode for many years with very few really knowing the soft Jacqui. But Jacqui didn't need someone to judge and talk down to her and tell her that this event didn't matter. 'That she was stupid making a fuss over nothing. Sure it was only an examination, it's you that's over reacting,' as I told myself, often.

I don't know when exactly I moved from judging and criticising myself, to being an advocate and friend. But I realised I didn't need to be destroying myself like that. My 15 year-old self needed someone to love her, to listen to her - not to judge her and instead step up and become an advocate for her. Be her voice because what was done was wrong and it was a violation on a child and it was time that the adult woman helped, loved and spoke for that 15 year-old.

As I write this book is about giving a voice to 15 year-old Jacqui, it shouldn't have happened and it mattered then and it matters now. That 15 year-old knew and knows that it was fundamentally wrong at many levels.

So I made a quality choice that love is a much more powerful tool to use in this process than judgement and fear. I love that my 15 year-old self tried to stop it but unfortunately he was going to perform the examination regardless of my questions and he knew as he proceeded with this so-called examination that he was violating and degrading me and in that moment taking my power of choice.

Going Home.

With each word and page I write I know that I am going home.

> "I have spent all of my life advocating for others.
> A life changing and inspiring moment was when
> I knew the time had come to advocate for me.
> Know that you are your greatest advocate.

Jacqui Taaffe

Lights The Way

INSPIRE HEAL EMPOWER

Quality Choices for me

I can continue to chase the Swamp man, however I choose to name him, but I know I'll never find him. I'll never get the sort of justice that I often thought of when I mention that word, in a Courthouse or from a Judge and jury of my peers, so I must create my own justice and I must decide that it is enough for me to acknowledge and recognise the deep hurt and violation I suffered at his hands.

I must make quality choices for me to move forward with my life and let go or give back all those numbing and dirty emotions I have carried within. They were never mine to carry and giving them back has been a powerful and healing process for myself.

Through drawing, visualisation and burning many of the notes that I have written has helped me release much internalised hurt. Freeing me and my wonderful essence to be who we are meant to be. When I speak of him he is like someone who has created the perfect crime. His presence or presenting himself as a doctor caused much confusion. But I know at my very core and essence this was not right, it was so wrong.

Do not underestimate the power of picking up your pen and writing down what flows through you. It's both healing and therapeutic. For you out there who sees yourself in this book, get out your pen and paper and start.

It took me a very long time to come to this point but the writing process has speeded up the flow of my thoughts and to see them looking back at me from the page once again reinforces that all these things, events, emotions and him – they are each separate to me and I can choose how I want to see things and choose what I can do in my life without my continuing to carry it.

Going Home.

With each word and page I write I know that I am going home.

Chapter Seven

It's not my story to keep

I have thought a lot about this. Why am I writing this? What is my intention? How will it affect my family and me? I am sure that for many of you with a similar story you may understand this and may have faced many of the same questions in your own life.

What is this force that pushes me to write these words and continue to write these words and write this book? I had no intention a year ago or six months ago to do this. But something keeps pushing me to write, to share my thoughts and feelings. Something at my core and essence is telling me that this must be shared with others. To not share it would be to further judge and deny what happened. For some strange reasons I keep hearing it's not just your story, it belongs to others too. So it is on that basis that I will write this and trust what happens next.

I have to make sure that sharing it comes from a space or a place to help others. My sharing these writings are in the hope that it allows others maybe to share theirs and I mean that even in the sense of sharing it with someone else. I told very few people as the time moved on and it was a thing or subject not to be spoken about – it became even harder to think about and mention. I do feel in my heart that I am one of many this has happened to yet it's like looking for a needle in a haystack to find someone else in the position I found myself in. So creating a space for that conversation or words that others may want to share is important. It was in meeting with Dignity4Patients in Drogheda where a staff member, Bernadette Sullivan, outlining some of the work that her organisation was doing that I heard myself say, 'sure that happened to me.' I said it out loud and so quickly – to be able to say to someone that something that I felt was quite wrong had happened to me – was so comforting. I never had a space in any conversation that really encouraged and allowed for me to share my story until that moment.

The organisation outlines their objective in the following way in their latest Annual Report 2019; 'Dignity4Patients was founded in 2008 and incorporated as a charity in 2010. Dignity4Patients has advocated on behalf of Irish patients for over a decade seeking support, recovery and justice for all sufferers of sexual abuse within the Irish Health service. Prevention of sexual abuse of patients is key to our work.'

Dignity4Patients in Drogheda do incredible work behind closed doors supporting and helping many. I have had many conversations and meetings with a key figure in the organisation, Bernadette Sullivan and she has never not been available either to speak on the phone to me or meet me. She has never made me feel that what had occurred to me was unimportant or didn't matter. She made me feel that my story mattered, that it was valued and I had never had that great support until 2013.

My husband was the only one I really would mention it to and he always listened and was there for me. He has supported me in any and all decisions I have taken. He always says to me that, 'you have to do what you feel you have to do for yourself.' That quiet, constant ear has been an incredible support to me over our 34 years together.

In the latest Annual Report 2019 from Dignity4Patients, Chair Paul Murphy sets the issue within a measured context as follows;

'Even a cursory perusal of media reports will show that sexual abuse in the health system is an ongoing problem that must be faced up to. The perpetrators are in the minority and the vast majority working in the health system have the care of their patients as their number one priority. But it is an established fact that patients continue to suffer sexual abuse or inappropriate sexual behaviour while in the care of medical and care services.'

In all, 217 of the 329 clients of Dignity4Patients sought and were given support, advocacy or information during 2019. For me that support was critical and I cannot imagine having to be put on a waiting list at the very moment that I had the courage to speak and come forward.

My motives in sharing my story are to create a safe space to have unspoken, difficult and hard conversations – without judgement, just to listen.

I started by listening to myself and I encourage you to do the same. In writing I allowed the flow of my pen to the page and allowed myself to no longer internalise. To write of my experiences without fear of judgement of me because as the saying goes, 'it is what it is.' To no longer internalise is to feel lighter in myself, in my heart. This story must be written and allowing my thoughts and feelings to rise to the tip of my pen is freedom in itself. Freedom that I am letting go or externalising what I previously felt was so much a part of me. It is not part of me and it never was, it was placed upon me and I internalised it, for many years trying to make sense of it. It no longer has a place within me and therefor it's time it became separate to me.

Withdraw

Why do I withdraw from life so much? I find calm and peace. It's strange but when I am the most unnerved, rattled and confused I must retreat to myself. My self is the safest place I can be. I must trust the fact that I have to withdraw and retreat. I know in my heart that others may not get that so these writings are for you. I don't mean to cause any judgement about myself. I simply need to withdraw and retreat.

I sometimes, well often, get that feeling of I must go home to the space and place that I am truly, wholly and absolutely me. The absolute that has always been there silently and waiting to guide me. When I am distant or quiet I simply need to go home. I encourage you to listen to that space and place in yourself.

Going Home.

With each word and page I write I know that I am going home.

TRUST
in the pursuit of'
"TRUTH"

When ones intention
is "Truth"
and to help others.
You become a magnet for
synchronicities
What once you thought
would be
unimaginable
"Appears"

Jacqui Taaffe ♥

Lights The Way

Chapter Eight

Cleaning Up

In trying to cope with the repressed memories, the shame and the swamp-like figure I channelled my shame and feelings into cleaning. I had to make things clean. I had to set things in order. Times you might say it became a compulsion. I have arrived at the view that cleaning for me was much more than the normal day to day household cleaning. Cleaning for me almost became therapeutic and a distraction from allowing myself to think. If I had so many things to clean and if I could make things sit perfectly then I felt that I had control, I have just realised that, as I write this part. I didn't see cleaning as a form of control but it is and it meant that I could control my thoughts, feelings and surroundings. Cleaning was for most of my adult life something that just had to be done in an ongoing daily routine from I opened my eyes until I went to sleep.

I would wake up around 5.30am and my cleaning regime would begin. First it was when I was still living at home before I moved out and got married. It would be relentless and I would get frustrated and upset if I had to fix stuff twice in the same day. It got harder to sustain when I got married and moved into my first marital home because I continued to maintain my Mum's home and now my own home too. You would be guaranteed to see me cleaning the front door and brass knocker every morning before I went to work.

There were multiple benefits for me in this behaviour, but overall they were distracting me from what I would have had to face if I dared stop – in other words THINK! To make sure that I wouldn't have time to think I chose to clean two houses and held a full-time job for 13 years running. I now realise how distracted I was and how much I was outrunning myself. Unconsciously I set the greatest task of all to outrun my thoughts and my feelings. Continually propelling myself from morning until night until my body was so tired it was safe to lie down and rest and sleep. I was so tired that I couldn't think.

When I stopped trying to outrun my mind, when I got still, when I stopped avoiding and became the watcher, observer and spectator of myself and my life rather than a participant or a runner in the race of it my whole life changed. I began to understand how cleaning was a coping mechanism to distract myself from what had happened. I was actually trying to cleanse or clean me from the dirt, grit and shame that I was carrying.

To keep my surroundings clean would in some bizarre way make me feel in control of myself and my surroundings which I didn't have on that day and in the moments of the sexual assault. The ongoing difficulty was that all the thoughts and feelings of shame and powerlessness were being still carried and suppressed within me. It would take me over 25 years but eventually and one pace at a time I stopped running and began facing into that fact. It is the empowering skills of coaching that has made all this happen for me.

So I stopped running and cleaning to the extent that I had been doing. I was amazed when I stopped running what I began to see. I don't need to scrub the house from top to bottom every day to feel clean. If I was to look back at my life, cleaning has been one of the healthier ways I chose to channel my sadness and loss of control and power that day. I clean now but not in the way I was compelled to clean before and I don't get frustrated and upset if something is not done or completed. I am more relaxed about it and can leave it.

Cleaning was very much tied to the idea of home and homeliness for me also. Although for over a quarter of a century my time spent cleaning and need to clean was certainly and in some ways out of balance, I did and do enjoy cleaning and being at home. Home, my house and being within my own four walls, has been important and essential for me all my life. Home for me is a space and place that I am safe, warm and at peace. I am me and I am so comfortable in my own skin when I am at home.

Now I am in a place where I have found home within - in my soul, essence and absolute. I want to help or guide others to their soul, essence and absolute home too. This feeling or sense of going home to self is the most peaceful, calm, safe, embracing environment to be in. In going within I have learned it has no judgement, no opinions, no advice, no suggestions, it is just there as a space of comfort and a real sense of home. This feeling is not found looking outside of myself for answers to my questions, it's simply there as the most whole feeling I have ever experienced without any of the distractions of life as I know it.

Home

Home is where myself is

Essence, soul, absolute.

Home is where myself - just

My pure self can be found.

Home is where I go to, when

I find myself losing my

Calm, my sense of self.

Home has everything I truly need,

It has simply just myself.

Myself is enough without any

Emotions, thoughts, ideas, opinions,

Judgements, beliefs that I have borrowed.

Myself is enough - within that

Enough is my absolute home.

Home is self simply.

-    Jacqui Taaffe, June 2020

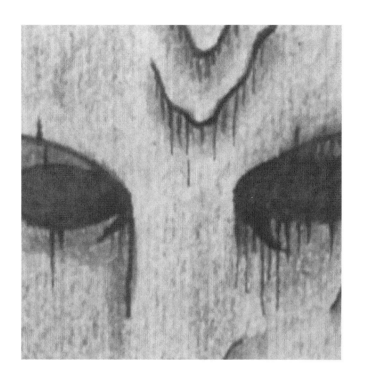

'That has been one of the greatest gifts and effects of taking the time to look at it, to seek the truth, to face the swamp-like figure and keep going.'

Illustration by Cian Lounds

Chapter Nine

My Right to Choose

I felt sad to realise that at the time of receiving my hospital records in 2014 that the only one this really, really mattered to was me. Now by that I mean that I was the only one who would ever have looked for them or understood that the so-called internal examination was definitely not officially recorded nor was the so-called breast check because they weren't written down in my hospital files. I was the only one who could have taken those steps, it was just me and I was doing it for my 15 year old self.

I have only spoken about this openly with a handful of people and the Garda. I have a right to choose now who I tell and how I tell my story. I choose how it is conveyed, how I share the truth and how it affected me. I choose to show him up for what he is, I choose to show this event up for what it was, I choose to no longer keep silent, I choose to say it and I choose to name it and I choose to ensure that I make choices that are inspiring, healing and empowering for me. I also hope that by breaking my silence and in sharing my story that I may help others.

Whilst my right to choose whether or not I wanted a so-called internal examination was taken from me on that day, my right to choose how I now see it and deal with it is mine. I can choose to stay drowning in the swamp of my suffocating, negative and gritty thoughts and feelings or I can choose to look at what I might take from this to strengthen my resolve for respect and dignity.

It's like a double-edged sword. On one side all the negative, grimy stuff which I cannot change, it is the residue of what happened and its only strength left now will be the attention, thought and feelings that I give to it. If I don't give that experience and the feelings any more attention it will I believe, in time, continue to fade. Fade may be too strong a word however I have found that I can detach myself from the event and I have found myself increasingly able to step back and stand away from it. That has been one of the greatest gifts and effects of taking the time to look at it, to seek the truth, to face the swamp-like figure and keep going.

I had the right to choose, I had the right to say No and I had the right to be heard on that day in the hospital. My right to choose was ignored.

The right to choose is vital to me. It is powerful and it is life-changing. It sounds too simple but when it is applied it can transform your life. Remember that the only two things under our control are our responses and reactions to external and internal noise, events and situations in our lives. Past actions or events cannot be changed but our power of choice always lies within us and how we choose to move forward in our lives. To be able to say – yes it happened but I will not let it define me.

My 15 year-old self was robbed of the right to choose. As I write these pages I have a real sense that it is that 15 year-old that is writing a lot of these words and together we are healing and being the best we have ever been to date. I am glad that the 15 year-old self is being shared and seen. No more need to hide in dark places – let's shine our light so bright that nothing can hide away, to shine as Beacons of Light.

On reflecting and looking back at the events of that day, 23 October 1984, I can't but notice how compliant I was with silence. How silent I was. I was not asked, my questions were not answered, I was not given the right of choice I was assaulted and it was done to me resulting in silence. How few people I told and how silent it all became. It was so silent that I became compliant with that silence too. This is one of the effects for me of being interfered with, of being assaulted - the removal of choice and the interruption of safety.

Maybe there was a piece of me that thought, sure if I don't talk about it and suppress it so deep in my mind, it will go away. But the observer, the absolute of my being embraced me until such a time arrived that both myself and the 15 year-old girl could break that silence. A silence that had been kept for over a quarter of a Century. I hope you can in some way understand how one can become so compliant with silence. Even now, as I write these words it (the sexual assault) really doesn't like me making any noise about it. That feeling in itself is strange.

Silence – Lie is found within the word silence, to keep it silent would be to keep the lie.

Silence can be no more, with words and noise comes conversations and space to make room for all the other good things that are to come. To create a safe space for the unspoken is far more empowering to oneself than retaining the lie within the silence.

I acknowledge that what happened, happened. But I have made a decision for my own mental health, that in acknowledging it happened I choose not to give it further value, power, attention or recognition.

I prefer to recognise and pay attention to how I handle it and give myself the acknowledgement and recognition of my own ability to rise from it. If I give that event any further recognition I would go down a road of giving it, in my opinion, a value and it holds zero value to me and my life. So I am deliberate in bringing my thoughts and feelings to a place where I can look at the event only in terms of how I am dealing with it now in this moment and that empowers me. I have chosen the safe and powerful place.

Knowing Choices

Powerful, incredibly powerful - we all have it. It's that part of me and that part of you that knows, that knows at your very core that something isn't right.

The BIGGEST choices I had to make from this event was either to ignore that very knowing within me that incredible power that each and every one has. Often - by no deliberate fault of anyone - we have not been taught nor encouraged to listen to and tap into it.

Choose to listen to me and that very knowing, a knowing that this cunning individual disguised as a doctor standing in front of me was not a doctor or medical person but a monster.

I CHOOSE ME. I choose to listen to myself. I choose to trust my feelings that what had happened was so wrong, so rotten and above all to make a choice for me and for my life that I will use these insights and information to inspire, heal and empower myself and others.

Going Home.

With each word and page I write I know that I am going home.

Consent

My right to say No mattered. My right to be listened to mattered. There is no fine line of consent, people have a right of choice and the right to say yes or no. There is no grey area when it comes to consent.

From my investigations as part of this process there weren't sufficient procedures and guidelines in place back in October 1984 that the hospital has been able to provide to me when it came to the care, dignity and respect of a minor or adult patient. There was no chaperoning policy or practice for minors, so I was left on my own. One would have assumed that my reaction and objection would have been respected and listened to and now I know of course that it wasn't even a legitimate procedure. My consent was neither wanted nor would it have mattered to someone set on assaulting me. So just reflect yourself please on this; I was fine when I thought I was having an examination of my eye. It was only when he said that he wanted or was going to do an internal examination that I said; 'I don't understand what that has to do with my eye.' He said; 'It has to be done.' So my power of choice to say no in that moment was taken away from me. I was left powerless and my dignity was taken and stripped.

There are guidelines now but I wonder are these guidelines enough to empower the voice of the patient to say No, to speak it out loud and have their right of that decision respected? Is there a clear guideline for children and minors so that they can be empowered to the best of their understanding and age to take power over that choice? I would like to start a conversation and make suggestions on how that might be improved and I am confident that as a society we can better protect vulnerable people and children.

That's something that matters to me - that each and every patient, regardless of age, has a clear guideline or map to follow which values and respects them and works at all times to respect and listen to their needs. I hope this book will trigger such conversations and help to open a space for such policies, guidelines and supports to be created.

Powerful incredibly powerful we all have it. It's that part of me and that part of you that knows that knows at your very core that something isn't right.

The BIGGEST choices I had to make from this event was either to ignore that very knowing within me that incredible power that each and every one of us has and by no deliberate fault of anyone we have not been taught or encouraged to listen to and tap into.

Choose to listen to me and that very knowing, a knowing that this cunning individual disguised as doctor standing in front of me was not a doctor or medical person but a monster.

I CHOOSE ME, to listen to me, to trust my feelings that what had happened was so wrong so rotten and above all to make a choice for me and for my life that I will use these insights and information to inspire heal empower me and other's.

Going Home.

With each word and page I write I know that I am going home.

Consent

The Right to Choose is vital to me and Consent must be both sought and given 100%. Informed consent is so important. Generally speaking, obtaining Informed consent means that a patient who agrees to undergo a treatment or procedure does so only after being made aware of the associated benefits, risks, and alternative treatments. I am suggesting that it goes further in pointing out exactly each step that will be involved and all of the treatments and procedures that a patient or minor is consenting to.

I am suggesting that the following recommendations be considered as additions to current Care of, Patient Consent and Safeguarding Policies and Procedures within medical settings.

The following recommendations would empower and educate both patients and staff and may narrow the opportunity of future abuse occurring in various medical settings.

I have called them the O'Brien recommendations in honour of my childhood self and birth name as I was Jackie O'Brien before I married and became Jacqui Taaffe.

The O'Brien recommendations:

1. Black and White Rule:

Consent has no grey area or room for misunderstanding and error in all the steps that must be taken to include, educate and inform the patient or minor of the process. Consent must be both clearly sought and clearly given. This recommendation would set out the steps involved in any admission or stay in hospital. The recommendation calls for patients to be clearly informed of each step and procedure that will be involved in a clear and timely manner and further would set scenarios that they would not expect without their written or witnessed consent being sought. I call this the black and white rule. Whereby it leaves no grey area, no doubt, no confusion and no misunderstanding for the person as to what to expect. I see this as a cornerstone in the safety of protecting the individual rights, their right to say no and dignity.

2. Last minute rule:

It is essential that the patient or minor knows that they have the power to choose. To say No or Stop. That at any time within reasonable notice the patient or minor has the right to stop any process, examination, treatment or procedure. They can make this choice without fear of prejudice or repercussion in the future.

3. Experience - Review Rule:

Here is an opportunity for the patient or minor to review and capture their experience within the hospital before or after discharge. This would be in the form of an evaluation of your experience as a patient and has the potential to remove the opportunity for error or wrongdoing to be hidden once again empowering the patient or minor by recognizing and valuing their experience. The Experience-Review rule has the potential to tighten and narrow opportunities for abuse to occur and be gotten away with and provide an environment that is supportive and reflective to minimise the potential for abuse to occur.

Source: Dignity4Patients Annual Report 2019

Patient Safety & Prevention: Engagement with State Bodies

To date Dignity4Patients under the supervision of a voluntary board has endeavoured to highlight the issue of Patient Sexual abuse to the relevant state bodies. However, the engagement and acknowledgement of the issue of sexual abuse of patients within the Irish Health Care system remains under the radar.

Public awareness, education and prevention needs to be improved.

It is our wish that at the start of a new decade in 2020 that Dignity4Patients is granted resources and opportunities to strengthen our engagement with Health and Justice Authorities and other allied agencies, to ensure adequate care for patients who have suffered sexual abuse and implementation of strong preventative measures.

There have been improvements in the safeguarding of vulnerable patients from abuse. It is our belief that all patients are vulnerable to sexual abuse because of patient dynamics and the nature of medical treatments and examinations. There have also been very welcome improvements for victims involved in criminal justice processes although it remains a very difficult process.

What is most needed is improved prevention measures together with improved care for patient victims both in the acute aftermath of suffering sexual abuse as a patient and in

Chapter 10

The Power of Enough

In letting go of what doesn't belong to me, of the choices and actions involved in the sexual assault on me, I came up against and still get times of huge resistance when it comes to giving it up and giving it back to him.

He not only brought in and left behind many self-limiting thoughts and doubts and emotions, he also tried to rob me of my self-esteem and my sense of being enough.

In letting go and giving up and giving back this manifestation of the swamp-like figure which was a combination of the thoughts, feelings and the emotions, I released a huge weight off me.

This book comes about because I have reached the point of enough is enough and no longer allowing myself to internalise my negative thoughts and emotions that arose from that experience and event.   To trust and allow the flow of my pen to the page. To write things without fear of judgement of me because as the saying goes, 'it is what it is.' To no longer internalise is to feel lighter in myself, in my heart. This story must be written and allowing my thoughts and feelings to rise to the tip of my pen is freedom in itself. Freedom that I am letting go, giving up and giving back what previously felt so much a part of me. It is not part of me and it never was, it was placed upon me and I internalised it in order to try to make sense of it. After some 36 years I can say that that sexual assault no longer has a place within me and therefore it is time it became separate to me and it is time for me to give it back.

Achieving this separation and becoming removed and able to observe the event from a wider perspective has been a game changer for me. To not be stuck in the situation and rather to be looking at it from a space of detachment enabled me to notice all the effects and impacts it was having. It empowered me to realise that I am in control and can choose which emotions and thoughts I want to continue to carry, hold or internalise. I made a choice that any that no longer help me, that make me feel small, inferior, helpless, limit me and hold me back had to go. In replacing them with the feelings that I choose to have I am healing and have stepped into being the person that I truly am – and have always been without this event ever happening to me.

I have allowed and I am uncovering a Powerful Me and she inspires me, is healing me and is empowering me to move forward as a beacon of light for others.

I had to first trust myself in order to find her, to become truly powerful I had to reach that point of enough. In becoming truthful and transparent with myself my first step was in taking the time to actually look at what had happened and stop the running and busyness with which I ran my life. Trust for me is a heart led emotion in other words it doesn't come from a thought I have. It comes from a feeling, a deep sense of knowing that it's okay or it's the right thing to do. Knowing, and in particular in my case, that regardless of how the individual showed up and how the circumstances may have appeared I knew and trusted at the very core of being that it was wrong.

Secondly, in speaking my truth for the very first time to a safe person I stepped forward on a new path. The Power of Enough meant for me clarifying what actually happened and what I needed to do to put this event in a place of peace. Writing my letters to the Hospital where the sexual assault took place allowed me to take my power back and to formally ask the biggest question of all for me; 'was the internal examination part of a minor's admission process to have an eye operation?'

I had taken control. Asking that question really summed up and captured what I had been searching for, that final clarity on any possibility that this had been a legitimate part of the admission process against my deep knowing that it could not have been. This answer for me was enough.

I survived and now with better knowledge and acceptance I am making conscious choices that empower me to rise.

In this book I have provided the tools that I have used and I share them in the hope that they will inspire you on your journey and that you too may find healing and empowerment to take back your power.

Trust

What is trust?

'Trust' is not a destination

You will not find 'TRUST' signposted with a set of directions.

You will not find 'TRUST' by listening to others.

'TRUST' is magical it's greater than the things you can see and touch.

'TRUST' is intangible.

'TRUST' cannot be touched nor seen, yet you KNOW when you feel it.

'YOU' know you have it – 'TRUST!'

'TRUST' gives you an incredible inner sense and feeling that it's ok and everything will work out.

'TRUST' is your inside gift available to you 24/7.

'TRUST' will be one of your most powerful and incredible advocates and guides.

Listen closely and attentively to it when it speaks to you. Above all 'TRUST!'

- Jacqui Taaffe

FREEDOM

FREEDOM is

Giving myself permission to speak my truth.

To give up all the doubts,

To give up all the thoughts,

To give up all the emotions,

To give up all the feelings,

To give up all the self-limiting beliefs,

And to call out and see things just as they are.

To give myself the greatest gift of all,

The FREEDOM to simply be me.

- Jacqui Taaffe

Trust and Being Enough?

I had to include Trust and being Enough because if I didn't trust and come to a place where I felt I was enough this book would not be written nor exist. When I placed trust, being enough and faith in my inner knowing, essence, core-intelligence, whatever you choose to call it - something wonderful began to flow from me. These words just started to appear on the pages with little effort or thought.

Placing trust, being enough and having faith in allowing this to happen allowed me to rise above and shed the layers of all the limiting beliefs that may stop each and every one of us living our lives on our own terms.

To trust that my story had to be shared, had to be enough for me. To trust that sharing my story might help someone else. This is my story and if by sharing it with you I help you in some way that's all that really matters. Its purpose is so simplistic and yet so powerful for me. To give my story a place whereby its pure intention is simply to help myself and others.

I must go to that place of trust and being enough every day to remind me that this is not about me. This is about something much bigger. But its core intention is pure and kind. To embrace others that may too have been sexually assaulted.

My message to you is trust – trust you, listen to that part of you that's ever present - your true self. Your true self is enough – Get to know it, embrace it, allow it to unfold and flow through you!

I AM ENOUGH

Going Home.

With each word and page I write I know that I am going home.

I Wonder

Oh I wonder what wonders would appear

If only for one day,
I wonder what magical creations
would appear

if one only listened to
and acted upon the part of
them that speaks from their heart.

Yes some call it soul,
whatever name you give it,
it is wonderful, full of wonder.

Oh I wonder what wonders would appear.

- Jacqui Taaffe

Chapter 11

Rising Choices

When a former work associate met me in Spring 2020 she voiced surprise for the second time in as many years at the changes that she saw in me, when I asked about her former view of me there is a common thread that runs through both her perception and experience of me. At an online event in May 2020 where I was giving the key presentation and overview of my work as a Life-Coach and speaking afterwards she voiced again in the online chat facility of the transformational change that she could see within me and how I had presented that day. Following a long working relationship in previous years I wanted to ask her and explore what she meant and how she had found me then, from the late 1990's on.

As a Life-Coach I know the power in asking the hard questions about yourself, getting the answers and learning from them without taking them personally or getting offended. This is a hugely powerful tool and the fact is that when we know better we can do better. I was really conscious of what I was asking my former work associate, I was asking her to be really honest and gave her permission by saying outright that I wasn't going to take her experience of me personally or get offended. I am delighted that she stepped forward and told me. This is what she said:

'In more recent times I find your presence calmer and lighter - that sense that I had of you that you were constantly on edge and tightly wound up like a springed-coil ready to unravel at any moment was gone. On first meeting you Jacqui I had a sense that I must choose what I said to you carefully as I felt that if I had said the wrong thing that you might jump in or un-coil.'

It's incredible how my protection mode and the suit of armour that I wore to protect me and used as a coping mechanism caused a sense of caution in others. A vibration that seems to have created a sense of needing to tread carefully around me. I could see and understand immediately what she had experienced, it wasn't a shock to me and I wanted to know so that I could understand myself better. Underneath that highly sprung exterior was a very fearful, vulnerable and a not good enough me. I know and I understand now more than ever that I wore that protection mode for years as a direct consequence of what had happened to me. I know now that there is no need to hide myself in that protective suit of armour. I need only to protect myself from now on from the old habitual thinking, feelings and default habits that I developed to hide my pain.

I say to you to trust in your inner essence and if it's telling you it's time to let go of the way you've got so familiar in living - again trust it and step into the unfamiliar. The freedom, lightness, calm and comfort I have experienced is worth the letting go of familiarity.

Rise! Shine your light brightly as a beacon of light. One of the labels that I have chosen is Beacon of Light because I don't believe that the labels often placed on someone like myself who has been sexually assaulted or abused, labels such as victim or survivor, empower us.

I am a Beacon of Light, I am shining a light on that dark place to expose it for what it was. I am telling everyone that I have nothing to be ashamed of and I will continue to encourage others to shine their beautiful light too. Together and talking, giving space to have that conversation - we are stronger.

My intention for these words and pages are to hopefully inspire, heal and empower you. These pages and this story is not to make you sad or sorry for me, these words are to share with you how I have taken a dark situation and flooded so much of my light into it that it has freed me.

All recognition must go to my 15 year-old self in how she navigated and dealt with the events of 23 October 1984. It has been a privilege for me to work through this with her and together to grow and uncover our strength, power and resilience. As the reader you might wonder why I talk about my 15 year-old self in the third person, this is because it empowers me through the deliberate intention to detach myself, so that I can look back and be the adult and make quality choices that heal both of us now.

Within the word resilience you will find the word silence and for me resilience is that silent champion within that keeps me getting back up and to keep going regardless of what comes at me or comes in my way is to be a silent champion to and a beacon of light for whoever I meet or come into contact with.

Resilience is the ability to keep bouncing back, to keep going regardless of how many knock downs and challenges I come up against in life. It is the ability to push and lift myself above whatever the obstacle or challenge is so that I can face it and overcome it on any given day.

On a daily basis I allow myself time to sit in silence with no preconditions, no expectations. I just trust the process, what I have found is that when I allow this silent space into my life it gives me guidance and the answers to many of the questions that I have and most importantly it gives me inner strength to keep going regardless. That strength feels like a magnet which then pulls and draws me towards what I want and what I know I have to do to stay true to me and who I really am.

Within that silent space there is great comfort, love, acceptance with limitless ideas, creativity, solutions and possibilities. In the silent space my 15 year old self and I can navigate and overcome self-limiting beliefs, dissolve unhelpful emotions and I am empowered to face the various challenges of life. It has enabled me to feel inspired and empowered to be who I truly am. Through sitting in silence regularly I have found myself guided and led to pursue education, knowledge and training to empower others through my Life-Coaching practice.

Each and every one of us can uncover our incredible resilience. Take note and pay attention that when I say resilience I bet that you know exactly and can describe what that means for you. And why is that, you might ask? Well that's because you know resilience and to know it is to have it. I ask you to remember that, in times when you doubt yourself, that resilience is part of you - please allow it space to talk to you.

Beacons

We are beacons of light and hope,

shining our light,

on dark places so they no longer hold

any power or hiding place.

I am nearly home,

home is where my heart is

and I am so happy

to go back there.

-    Jacqui Taaffe, 2020

INSPIRE HEAL EMPOWER

A path less traveled is not without
it's challenges & struggles but what it
continually gives you back is a
complete sense of
"Freedom" to be oneself.

Jacqui Taaffe

Lights The Way

149

I am Resilience

I am

I am all the things

I was before it happened,

And I am all of

These things now.

I am kind

I am honest

I am intuitive

I am knowing.

I am incredible

I am powerful

I am resilient.

I am accepting

I am trust

I am truth

I am enough.

- Jacqui Taaffe, 2020

Rising

How do you rise from such events?

By becoming separate from them,

By becoming an observer of them,

By looking at it -

Rather than looking from within it.

When I am within it, I am powerless, struggling and attempting to rationalise the irrational.

When I am separate?

I don't have that heaviness and powerlessness that belongs to him.

I don't have to rationalise his actions.

They are not mine to rationalise, they belong to him.

If I was to go further – I would say that this separateness of myself to the events places me in a powerful position, in a position to see the truth of the situation.

To choose what I want to choose from it.

Rather than allowing any thoughts and emotions of these events to be imposed on me. I choose how I rise from this – untouched, unblemished. Let go, along with him, all of the thoughts and emotions he brought to that day through his actions.

Let go I say and so I rise from it.

Going Home.

With each word and page I write I know that I am going home.

Chapter 12

Enough is Enough

At some stage I had to decide what I was searching for to fulfil me and get closure on this entire event. I have arrived at the conclusion that I will never find the person who did this and I will never succeed in holding him directly accountable for his actions.

'When is Enough, Enough?

When I believe, I am enough!'

However knowing that an internal examination was not part of my admittance process for my eye operation, as a minor, is enough. As it stops me and gives me clarity that indeed this internal examination was nasty and wrong. I don't need anyone else to believe that this occurred I only need to know that this happened and that it shouldn't have. Clarification around that gives me the freedom to let it go and give all the nasty back to the person who brought it to me. My deep knowing is enough for me.

I trust that these things will take care of themselves. I know for a fact that my essence is taking care of me. The power to let go of all the limitations I placed on myself for many years and give back all the nasty baggage that was left with me that day, has been a liberating experience. I am not that event and it does not define me.

What defines me is who I am now and where I go next. Not needing outside approval, acceptance and belief from others is incredibly powerful.

Justice is not always delivered in a Court Room or in any official sense that many may think of as justice. I took my control back and I found my own inner justice on the day that I received the letter from the Hospital Chief in June 2020 confirming that neither an internal examination nor a breast check were ever part of the admittance process for my eye operation. So justice can come in many forms and I have found consolation and validation through this recognition from the hospital and seeing it written down in black and white in a sentence. The value and comfort of that one sentence can't be measured or put into words. That one sentence is so invaluable to me because it brought my doubt and my knowing together and when doubt meets knowing all that can remain is knowing.

That knowing is enough for me.

If I were to allow my mind to continue to torture me with ifs and buts and what I should've done I would deliver to myself a great injustice. I did my best as a 15 year-old child and now allowing that child to forgive herself and how she handled it back then is powerful. I hug her and tell her now in my mind:

'You did the best with what you knew. You were sexually assaulted.

You were strong and resilient in the years that followed - how incredible you are!'

Written a few weeks after receiving the Hospital letter

I am happy

For the first time in years this morning I feel a happiness within that empty and lonely place that I and my 15 year-old self has carried. Why? Because the doubt is gone – I know - I really, really, really know that what I always knew is true. That is that it was not an official examination, it should not have happened and now I have confirmation for myself.

I feel happy that I am writing these pages and sharing my deepest and darkest thoughts. I am not alone.

It's strange to see light going into that empty and dark and lonely place my 15 year-old self first created to hide that monster - that the swamp like figure. The beacon of light is shining on it and it's making me peaceful. I am strangely at peace this morning with myself.

Going Home.

With each word and page I write I know that I am going home.

In Closing – Author's Note

So as we come to the end of this book my intention is that I may have provided some insights through sharing my journey, the lessons that I have learned and how I have overcome its obstacles. I have hopefully shown you that it's empowering to be vulnerable, open, honest and transparent in sharing difficult stories.

My wish is that this book and these words might resonate with you and that you may find inspiration, healing and empowerment.

Reach out to me if you ever doubt yourself, lack confidence or struggle with your thinking and would like to create peace of mind, happiness and meaning in your life.

Here are my 10 key takeaways:

1. Thoughts – you are not your thoughts let them pass by knowing that at any moment you can choose your thoughts.

2. Begin to regulate your thoughts with thoughts that will place you in a state of gratitude and happiness.

3. You become what you think about and tell yourself - choose wisely, choose kind and encouraging thoughts.

4. Pay attention to the conversations you have with yourself and ensure that they are kind and helpful – know that you can change the conversation. Believe me if you practice this repeatedly it works.

5. Doubt is one of the biggest barriers to people living a full life and following what inspires them in their heart. Embrace the doubt but tune into that part of you that knows, tune into that instinctive intuitive part of you that knows, trust it and follow your heart. You can choose from this moment on to be the person that you want to be.

6. Get a journal or a notebook and get writing. There are no rules – these are your private thoughts so just allow the pen to touch the paper and let them flow.

7. Look at starting a practice of daily meditation, don't knock it until you try it for at least 30 days. There are many meditation apps available that may help you.

8. Surround yourself with people, animals, nature and things that make you happy, things and people that energise you and lift your spirits.

9. Trust that similar people will gravitate towards you and accept that some may fall away.

10. Start a gratitude practice and list at least three things that you are grateful for every morning and night.

An Almost Final Word

Why did I write this book?

To light the way. I listened and trusted to my true self – my inner knowing and deep intelligence within and I sought answers and closure.

It is my hope that by sharing my story others might find answers also.

I am asking Society to reflect and consider how we might strengthen the policies and procedures around patient care and safeguarding plus further empower patient consent practices.

I am asking Society to reflect and reconsider the labels given to anyone who has come out the other side of sexual assault. We are each - 'Beacons of Light.'

My intention is to inspire, heal and empower.

You are incredible, you are determined, you are passionate. You are infinite. You have so much power within you to do anything you decide to do.

Dare to fly and soar to the heights that you are designed for.

YOU ARE INDEED, MY FRIEND, INCREDIBLE!

With Raw
Courage Determination
&
Passion
She Flies!

Jacqui Taaffe ♥

Postscript

In the final days of creating this book, that stage back in November 2020 where every single word mattered and was being considered and as I read through and looked set to finish the book something incredible happened that has reinforced for me why I wrote this book and why you should trust in yourself.

Why I had to write it.

You see when I started this book I had to write it down, I had to tell my story. I also believed that there must be others.

I never believed that it was just me.

I wanted to share my story so that anyone else with the same experience would know that they were right all along and that out there someone would believe them and understand.

It was a sense of knowing that drove me to write this book, the type of book that I wish I had been able to find and read when I started my journey.

And then it happened – all at once – I received a phone call that would confirm that I am not on my own.

Truth has found a way. That phone call was one of the most important of my life, amongst the profound sadness that there are indeed others. If I hadn't gone through the process of writing this book I would never have known. I hope this book finds you. I set the intention to write this book for us.

I wish you healing and I am here if you would like to reach out to me or to Dignity4Patients.

Please contact Dignity4Patients.org Telephone: 00353 41 984 3730 Text: 00353 86 165 4111 Email: support@Dignity4Patients.org

With Love

Jacqui Taaffe

Acknowledgements

I want to thank the following people and groups who have joined me along the journey of bringing this book into the world!

Pat Taaffe, my husband, who I first met in 1987 and who has been by my side ever since. Pat is a true partner and has supported me in a way that has allowed me to follow the process of writing this book and establish my business, JT Coaching. I am so grateful to Pat every day for giving me the space to do this and for temporarily taking on everything else - all the other stuff of life!

Kara Taaffe, my daughter - gifted, kind and creative and for her eye art image and her incredible advice; Mum you know that people will judge you. But what's more important is you share your story to help others.'

Bernadette Sullivan for her constant support and guidance over the past 9 years and to the Board and Management of Dignity4Patients. Dignity4Patients.org Telephone: 00353 41 984 3730 Text: 00353 86 165 4111 Email: support@Dignity4Patients.org

Rape Crisis Centre Services - thank you.

Heather Shields, Editor, for being there for me all the way throughout this emotional roller coaster process.

Breda Marron, Irish Soul Artist, friend and a colleague for my incredible soul art painting which is the cover of this book, INSPIRE, HEAL, EMPOWER.

Marina Branigan, Brava Virtual, friend and colleague for her incredible support and PA work for my INSPIRE HEAL EMPOWER toolkit included within this book.

Cian Lounds, Illustrator, a talented artist and illustrator for his incredible swamp like figure and eyes images, with and without scalpel.

Andrea McQuillan, Web Developer and Director at Coppertops Digital Marketing Ltd for website design and pre-order page for Inspire, Heal, Empower.

Donna Kennedy for her time and an enlightening conversation in which she told me to go and that she believed I could 'SHINE.'

Clare Copas, PCdp MonClare Data Protection Consultancy. Clare's professionalism is incredible. She is a joy to know and work with.

Pat Slattery for his mentorship and the members of The Outstanding Network – YOU ARE INCREDIBLE!!

Charles C Finn for permission to print his wonderful poem 'Please Hear What I'm Not Saying' which holds so much meaning for me. PoetrybyCharlesCFinn.com

The Irish Times for permission to reprint excerpts from the article 'Ireland, 1984: A year of fierce debates and 'mounting evils' by Rosita Boland', first published July 7 2019.

Last and by no means least to my 15 year old self thank you so much Jackie O'Brien we have been through some process and journey.

I AM MY GREATEST ADVOCATE!

We are truly home now.

This book is for you, my 15 year old self

and all the Others.

INSPIRE, HEAL, EMPOWER TOOLKIT

TOOL ONE:

INSPIRE – HEAL – EMPOWER DAILY PRACTICES

Some principles I encourage you to deeply reflect upon and to adopt as a daily practice.

1. The only things in our control are how we react and respond.

2. At any given moment, we have the power to CHOOSE and the ABILITY to rewrite our stories.

3. My experience and the aim of the trauma for me was to keep me silent, undermine and degrade me through a continuous torrent of negative limiting self-talk, limiting beliefs and nasty feelings and to make me doubt and question myself. So pay attention, become aware of your inner chatter and see it for what it is – then choose to be the incredible self that YOU ARE!

4. The past is the past. Use it for reference purposes only.

5. When it comes to creating our stories, it takes many parts and elements to come together to create it. We need to be the narrator, producer and editor, to name only a few of the roles. You play of all those roles in your own life stories and it's within those roles you play that your power lies – to create the life stories you want.

6. You can be your biggest advocate and supporter in the stories you create. Listen to and trust yourself from your heart space. Choose the stories that will inspire, heal and empower. If at times you find you have to review and edit stuff, then so be it. That's what's incredible about being a human. You Are Incredible!

Human beings are incredible storytellers. We create stories from each and every interaction we have with others. Some of those stories can be untrue, can upset us, belittle us, keep us stuck and not help us to be the incredible individuals that we truly are.

When it came to me truly overcoming my traumatic life event, I had to **recognise** that I'd created a story that day about myself and what had happened.

By becoming aware of and **CURIOUS** about the story I had created that day around that event, I shone a big light on all of those untrue thoughts, beliefs and labels I had placed on myself. I chose to take control and change them.

Giving back the parts of that story, all of the nasty untrue thoughts, beliefs and feelings to their rightful owner has been hugely healing and empowering for me.

Rewriting my thoughts, beliefs, feelings and labels has inspired, healed and empowered me to overcome this event.

There Can Be Many Perspectives to a Story

In the case of the story I created that day about my life traumatic event there were two sides.

One side of the story had an incredible constant, empowering belief. This empowering belief has been constantly with me, an unshakable, knowing in my heart that the internal examination I had undergone that day was wrong. 36 years later, that empowering belief has brought me to writing this book and sharing my tools today.

The other side of the story, which I now know to be the untrue part, the part that I carried for the years which told me I didn't matter, that I was stupid and that minimised the events of that day.

But with the knowledge, education and skills I have learned over the past number of years, I started to believe and know better about myself. I recognised that I could rewrite the parts of that story which kept me silent and compliant for 36 years.

I recognised that stepping outside of myself, I could become the observer, the watcher of me. That I could control, choose and create a set of thoughts, beliefs and labels that would inspire, heal and empower me.

In my toolkit you'll find really valuable, practical information about thinking, thoughts, self-talk, limiting and empowering beliefs, observer or watcher and labelling.

If any of the content or tools that I have created to overcome, inspire, heal and empower myself from my own personal traumatic life experience resonate with you, please use it in your own life.

Fact: Things to know about thoughts

- **Thinking** is a collection of thoughts and the quality of a person's thinking is directly connected to the quality of their thoughts or self-talk.

- Every person has between **60,000** and **80,000** thoughts per day. Most of these thoughts are repetitive – just like an old record that's stuck on repeat and just keeps replaying. All of the studies show the incredible number of thoughts that we each experience daily.

- Studies show that when you create a new thought, you actually rewire your brain. The more you practice creating new thoughts, the more the same neurons will learn to work together and wire together.

As neuroscientists say, neurons that fire together, wire together.

So directed, willed attention and deliberate thinking can clearly and continually alter the brain function.

- Thoughts come from a collection of things we've experienced over the course of our lives; events, situations, things that we hear in passing or that are said to us and things that happen to us.

- The type of self-talk we have, whether it is empowering (positive) or disempowering (negative) is a direct reflection of our thoughts. When it came to overcoming my traumatic life event, controlling and choosing my self-talk was the key to me feeling good about myself.

- If your mood is not good or helpful, it's likely that your self-talk is disempowering. Begin to pay attention to what your self- talk is saying and make a choice to replace it.

Thoughts are just passing things and nothing else.

They are not who you are - they only become powerful if you believe them.

Thoughts Tool

1. **Make yourself a promise** that from today on You Will Choose to Believe Only Thoughts That Will Inspire Heal Empower.

2. **Become aware of your thoughts** and pay close attention to your self-talk. This will put you in a position to start the practice of creating thinking that not only will empower you but will heal and inspire you too.

   Gentle Reminder – Thoughts flow through our minds. We can't stop them. **Let Them Flow / Watch Them** by paying attention and becoming aware of your thoughts.

3. **Choose you first.** By choosing Inspiring, Healing and Empowering Thoughts over disempowering thoughts, you are choosing to look after yourself.

   a) **Write** down your thoughts. Be aware of the negative thoughts.

   b) **Recognise** that they are just thoughts.

   c) Look at the thoughts on paper.

d) Separate the thoughts under the headings Empowering / Disempowering and list them.

e) **Give up** the disempowering thoughts.

f) **Control** and **choose** the empowering thoughts.

g) **Read** through the empowering thoughts and FEEL them.

h) **Notice** how the empowering thoughts make you feel.

Gentle reminder – Thoughts are made up of a collection of words, words are made up of a collection of letters and you can choose to create a collection of letters which will form words and thoughts that inspire, heal and empower you.

4. **Repeat** the practice daily, until the day arrives – and it will – that the practice itself becomes part of you.

Here are some of the inspiring, healing and empowering thoughts on my list:

I am enough

I am strong

I am the master of my life

I am taking steps each day to improve my mind-set

I am self-mastery

I am in charge of my self-talk

I am incredible

I am kind

I am honest

I inspire myself by choosing to do what's best for me.

I am a great mum

I am friend

I love me and I like me

If you choose to do above actions, I guarantee you that in time you will re-program how you think. The mental health habits and wellbeing benefits you'll gain from this practice are limitless.

They will INSPIRE, HEAL AND EMPOWER YOU!

Gentle reminder – You are INCREDIBLE! Keep your promise to yourself today and every day that you will be **open-minded and committed** from now on to doing this practice by deliberately choosing your thoughts.

To use the analogy of a house when it comes to human thinking:

If the structure of a house and its foundations are not built correctly, eventually the house will start to have problems and in time, if not addressed, the entire structure may fall. When it comes to human thinking, the quality of a person's thoughts and self-talk are the master key to living a peaceful, happy and fulfilled life.

Thoughts are the foundation that hold the entire person together and with the right information, tools and a willingness to try them, that person will transform their life.

You Are Your Greatest Advocate!

This INSPIRE, HEAL, EMPOWER toolkit is adaptable

TOOL TWO:

OBSERVING

What does it mean to be an observer of you?

Being an observer of yourself requires that you become aware of your thoughts, feelings, emotions and behaviours.

When in this state of mind, you can process information differently. It's like watching yourself on a TV screen.

When I became an observer of myself it was a life changing moment. It gave me the ability to take a higher vantage point to look at my challenging life events from a higher perspective and different angles.

Becoming the observer of myself, the watcher of my own thoughts and self-talk has completely empowered and transformed my life. It has allowed me to stay separate and let go of self-limiting thoughts and emotions I carried from that day which did not belong to me.

It has allowed me to detach, let go of the thoughts and emotions I carried from that day which did not belong to me.

Being an observer allowed me to metaphorically step outside of myself to look back objectively, clinically at the events that day as an outsider, not as a 'victim.'

185

There is something incredibly empowering, healing and transformative about being able to step outside of one's self, detach and mentally separate oneself and look back at the event as a spectator or watcher.

As an observer/spectator, I can look at the events of that day both clinically and methodically because I am separate and outside of the confusion, thoughts and emotions that internally were stirred and arose within me from the day and which, at the time, I was completely immersed in.

I can ask myself questions which will give me clarity to the truths and untruths of that day and allow me to discover what does or doesn't belong to me.

Being an observer gives you the power of choice to make empowering quality choices and knowing that.

Now that I can observe my thoughts and notice what emotions they stir; I can CHOOSE what empowering thoughts and emotions I want to take forward with me. I can choose to either give them up or give them back.

The only two things under your control are your reactions and responses – both to internal and external noise.

Now, knowing that at any moment I have the power within me to choose how I react and respond to each and every element of my life, and in the case of that specific day and traumatic life event, I choose to give recognition and credit to the 15-year-old girl – me, myself and I – for how, together, we have handled the impact and aftereffects of that day.

Being an observer gives you the POWER to GIVE UP or GIVE BACK

For me it has been both healing and empowering to Give Up or Give Back the thoughts, beliefs and emotions which I carried from that day back to the perpetrator. Sitting and working slowly through exactly what belonged to me that day which has freed me from the untruths.

This practice has enabled me to rewrite and reframe that event.

I believe that when you know better, you can do better. I have and I continue to grow and evolve.

Observer Tool

Ask yourself, 'What am I carrying from this event that no longer belongs to me?'

Write them down...

<table>
<tr><td></td></tr>
<tr><td></td></tr>
<tr><td></td></tr>
<tr><td></td></tr>
<tr><td></td></tr>
<tr><td></td></tr>
<tr><td></td></tr>
</table>

<table>
<tr><td></td></tr>
<tr><td></td></tr>
<tr><td></td></tr>
<tr><td></td></tr>
<tr><td></td></tr>
<tr><td></td></tr>
<tr><td></td></tr>
</table>

Either let go, give up or give back.

Choose You what's best for YOU. Make a choice to lay-down and let go what you no longer need to carry.

This INSPIRE, HEAL, EMPOWER toolkit is adaptable

TOOL THREE:

BELIEFS

Within every set of circumstances, interactions, conversations – or in my case, a traumatic life event – we create a set of stories. Within these stories, we create sets of beliefs. Now, some beliefs are helpful and empowering but there are beliefs that also limit us, hold us back and stop us from living full lives. We unknowingly prevent ourselves from fulfilling our potential if we take those beliefs as fact.

I lived for a long time before I became aware of my belief system and learned more about it, but when I did it was a life changing moment.

It has positively empowered me in all areas of my life right now. In particular it has played a crucial part in me overcoming my trauma. It enabled me to look for facts within the events of that day, to search for and find the lies within the beliefs that I had carried from that day.

What are belief systems?

We all have a belief system. Belief systems are the stories we tell ourselves to define our personal sense of reality. It is through our belief system that we 'make sense' of the world around us.

Belief systems are made up of:

- Self-limiting beliefs – assumptions or perceptions that you've got about yourself and about the way the world works. These assumptions are 'self-limiting' because in some way they're holding you back from achieving what you are capable of.

- Empowering beliefs – beliefs that we have about ourselves which are helpful, positive and accurate. Empowering beliefs give us power because they affect our thoughts, feelings and actions. They help us to take positive action and feel good about ourselves.

Each of us has a set of 'CORE Beliefs' which are basic beliefs about ourselves, other people, and the world we live in.

It's my mission to shine a light the on facts of all my stories and to find the untruths and untruthful beliefs that can kept me stuck within that story. To share with you the tools to do the same.

I am the inspiring and empowering creator of my stories.

Know that with this valuable information and knowledge, you can dismantle and rewrite your stories too.

Find the Facts vs. Lies Exercise

Remember the 4 R's: Recognise – Rub it Out – Replace – Repeat

Know that you have two types of belief systems – **Self-limiting beliefs and Empowering beliefs** – choose a story that you have told yourself.

Recognise

Write down the both sets of beliefs you have about the story under the appropriate headings.

Examples of **self-limiting beliefs** – I am too old, I am too young, I don't have enough time, others would be better than me at doing that, I wouldn't be able to do that on my own, I am not good enough, I don't know where to start, I am stupid, I don't matter.

Examples of **empowering beliefs** – I am intelligent, I have valuable life experiences, I am kind, I am loyal, I am trustworthy, I have a lot to give, I am a good friend, I am loving, I am brave, I AM INCREDIBLE!

Self-limiting beliefs	Empowering beliefs

Facts vs. Lies

Ask yourself, is that self-limiting belief true? Is there a **lie** within it?

If you believe it to be fact, go on a fact-finding mission to back it up.

If you see it for the lie that it is, **rub it out**. You can either scribble over it or rub it out completely.

Now, rewrite an empowering belief to **replace it**.

Repeat – Repeat - Repeat

In the case of my story, I believed from the events of that day that I didn't matter. That I wasn't good enough. That I was stupid. Those limiting beliefs held me back in various ways and one that really jumps out at me was the limiting belief that I was stupid because I wasn't clever enough to stop the examination that day. That limiting belief was and is simply untrue. As a consequence of that limiting belief, I didn't take risks, chances or specific opportunities in life.

Now, because I know better, I choose to be and do better!

This INSPIRE, HEAL, EMPOWER toolkit is adaptable

TOOL FOUR:

LABELS

The fourth part of the toolkit is to highlight labelling and create further awareness about how labels can limit us and conform us in our lives and, in particular, labels used or related to a traumatic life event.

The following are my thoughts, opinions and ideas with regard to labelling. They are in no way expressed or intended to offend or hurt anyone. Particularly survivors and victims because they are the champions, advocates and beacons of light in my view.

The purpose of this section is to get you thinking about labels and how we use them in society. Just because something is that way, it doesn't mean it shouldn't be looked at, reflected upon and considered. What if we imagined considering different labels and how those labels might empower and inspire individuals? I wonder, what if?

What are labels and how do we use them?

Sometimes labels can help us. They can enable us to create a clear mental picture. They can help us to establish trust, rapport and expectations of what behaviours we might expect from ourselves and others. If we think of the word 'teacher', for example, we will conjure up a mental image and a set of qualities that we believe the label carries.

This is the same for every other label used.

<u>Attention</u>

Become aware of the labels you place on yourself. They can be empowering or self-limiting on your thoughts, behaviours and the actions you take.

I encourage you to pay CLOSE attention to the labels that you place on yourself every day.

Choose labels about yourself that recognise and acknowledge how unique and incredible you are. Do not hesitate in changing those labels if you feel and believe that they are not empowering and appropriate to you.

The next time you label yourself, I encourage you to pause and ask yourself if that label is self-limiting you in any way. If it is, CHANGE IT to an empowering label.

Reflection

Intentionally or unintentionally labelling in any form places preconceptions and limits on a person. It can often box us in, metaphorically speaking. I know for the purposes of living in this world they are useful, but I encourage you to question the benefit of some of those labels. In particular, I would ask you to reflect on the labels of 'victim' and 'survivor'. Ask yourself the following questions:

What comes to mind for you when you hear those labels?

What mental image do you create in your mind of them?

What category would you see those labels under i.e. empowering or limiting?

What benefits do you see for the individual by labelling them those names?

What are your thoughts on reconsidering those labels?

What would you see as an empowering label for individuals who been affected by a challenging life event?

My Story – My Labels

When it came to my inappropriate medical examination (sexual assault), I never labelled myself. That was not an intentional choice at the time, but looking and reflecting back on it, not labelling myself and **stepping on and out of it** has helped to empower me. I believe that if I'd labelled myself, it would have limited my thinking and conformed me.

I believe that I wouldn't be writing what I have written today if I hadn't stepped *on* those labels rather than *into* them.

I choose to believe that 'victims' and 'survivors' are BEACONS of light, whose life journeys have been interfered with or interrupted. I believe in giving people recognition and acknowledgment, dignity and respect for how resilient, brave and courageous they are.

They are incredible!

Remember that, at any time, you have the power to choose.

You *define* **you.**

You have the power to choose your labels.

Choose the ones that will empower and inspire you.

Who matters most? You do – and what's most important is what you think of you.

JT Coaching's Self-Mastery Tip:

Focus your attention and energy on becoming an authority on yourself.

Choose you to inspire!

This INSPIRE, HEAL, EMPOWER toolkit is adaptable

TOOL FIVE:

FORGIVENESS (LETTING GO)

There is a hidden message within the word forgive (for-give). It tells us that, whatever you are struggling with, it's not **for** you to keep forever it's to **give** up. Let it go to allow space for the new things and energy to come into your life.

Forgiving yourself and others is one of the most resilient and empowering acts of self-care you can choose to do. It frees up space and positive energy for new things to come in because holding on to what doesn't help you keeps you stuck.

Wrap yourself with the same kindness and consideration you give to others.

Benefits of Forgiveness (Letting Go):

1. Forgiving yourself ignites the healing process, being kind to yourself the way you are to others allows a new way of being with yourself.
2. Forgiveness and acceptance of what is, rather than focusing on what you wanted it to be, brings peace of mind.
3. Forgiving yourself is a courageous act of self-care. It's not for faint-hearted as you will have to leave behind thoughts and emotions which in turn will take you to new way of being.
4. Forgiveness frees your attention to what you can heal and what you can control going forward.
5. Forgiveness of oneself is a pure act of love.
6. Forgiveness brings opportunity to move on with your life.
7. Forgiveness brings solutions and a resilient mind-set.
8. Forgiveness enhances your overall wellbeing and self-belief.
9. Forgiveness places you in the driving seat of your life.
10. Forgiveness give you the freedom to begin many new and healthy lifestyle and wellbeing choices.
11. Forgiveness is your path to magical inner peace.
12. Forgiveness enables you to let go of, give up or give back negative energy.
13. Forgiveness invites an incredible empowering energy in.
14. Forgiveness opens the door the new beginnings and ways of being.

Forgiveness Tool

New Rules, New Choices, New Ways of Being

1. **Recognise/Include YOU**
   a. Reflect on and write down how you treat others. Then, make a choice to deliberately include yourself in that image from now on.

2. **Be Gentle**
   a. Why are we so hard on ourselves? Let it go. Love Yourself!

3. **See Challenges as Opportunities**
   a. Embrace life's challenges as opportunities to grow and lessons to learn. These are your moments to be your greatest ADVOCATE.

4. **Love Your Imperfections**
   a. Adopt the attitude of loving your imperfections. When you got here, you arrived with everything you needed for this journey. There is a message within the word **IM-PERFECTION – I'M PERFECT**.

It's okay to say, 'I LOVE me. I LIKE me and I forgive myself.'

It's okay to say, 'I am kind and loving.'

It's okay to say those things and, most importantly, to mean them.

There is one person that each and every one of us cannot escape from and that is ourselves.

It's time to give ourselves love and forgiveness.

Forgiving yourself is the greatest act of self-love you can do for you.

Gentle Reminder:

Each moment is an opportunity to write your new inspiring, healing and empowering story.

This INSPIRE, HEAL, EMPOWER toolkit is adaptable

I Must Be Obedient to the Callings of My Soul!

To be my truest self, to find calm, fulfilment and peace of mind,

I must listen to and be obedient to the callings of my soul.

To be Whole

To find my true meaning

I must listen to and be obedient to the obedient of my soul.

For if I am not to listen I will only be a shadow of myself.

I must listen to and be obedient to the callings of my soul.

To the callings of my 'TRUTH'

To who I am

To what I am

To what I am here to do.

I must RISE above my fears, worries and doubts.

To be able to go to that safe place within me that has everything I need,

I must listen to and be obedient to the callings of my soul.

I must be obedient and trust the callings of myself.

Yes I choose to be obedient and to listen to the callings of my very soul,

So at last I have found myself truly at home!

- Jacqui Taaffe ♥

Self-Empowerment

'I believe and know that self-empowerment can only be truly achieved by becoming knowledgeable, curious and understanding of oneself.

To become an authority & expert on yourself.

Self-Empowerment is Self-Knowledge.'

My mission is to inspire, heal & empower many by enabling them to become their own expert. If you are struggling, feeling stuck, worrying, anxious, lacking confidence and doubting yourself well then it's time to reach out and work with me.

I did not just become more confident, I didn't get confidence either.

I became confident because I became an authority and expert on myself.

That's what I do when I work with clients, they become their greatest authority and expert also so that they can be, do and have the life that what they want.

That's how you can and will overcome any of your life challenges. Remember that all you have and need is within you.

I believe and know that without doubt Self-Empowerment is Self-Knowledge

Let's talk, contact Jacqui at JacquiTaaffe.com

Printed in Great Britain
by Amazon